JANEY'S ARCADIA

JANEY'S ARCADIA

Errant Ad^ent$res in Ultima Thule

RACHEL ZOLF

Coach House Books
Toronto

first edition

Canada Council for the Arts Conseil des Arts du Canada

Canada

Published with the generous assistance of the Canada Council for the Arts and the Ontario Arts Council. Coach House Books also acknowledges the support of the Government of Canada through the Canada Book Fund and the Government of Ontario through the Ontario Book Publishing Tax Credit.

LIBRARY AND ARCHIVES CANADA CATALOGUING IN PUBLICATION

Zolf, Rachel, author
Janey's Arcadia / Rachel Zolf.

Poems.
ISBN 978-1-55245-295-0 (bound).

I. Title.

PS8599.O627J35 2014 C811'.54 C2014-904397-X

Janey's Arcadia is available as an ebook: ISBN 978 1 77056 393 3

Purchase of the print version of this book entitles you to a free digital copy. To claim your ebook of this title, please email sales@chbooks.com with proof of purchase or visit chbooks.com/digital. (Coach House Books reserves the right to terminate the free digital download offer at any time.)

'Genealogy is grey, meticulous and patiently documentary. It operates on a field of entangled and confused parchments, on documents that have been scratched over and recopied many times.'

– Michel F@lkOde

CONTENTS

JANEY'S INVOCATION

Infallible settlers say this is the latest season
they have known. All seed life seems somnolent,
yet a delicate suggestion of colour is at the tips
of the willows. An insidious, slow-moving process
is at work in the trees – one that spells from death
-car to drive more slowly unto drouth-world. The wine
of spring aflush on the face THE COPS- FIND- 2 J3<3
I H • ^ \ Hn is a Goad of Death Gourd of chanqts Takt
Life is totally totally lonely of Nature. Dearth is
the only reality we've got left in our nicey-nicey-
clean-ice-cream-TV scraps, so we'd better worship
the long wall of skulls next to the ball park. The delay
only whets our monstrosity. A unique beauty about
this pre-vernal landscape before it is screened
by red-brown colour, air and surface, semi-thick –
a boldness suggestive of how Janey and the rest
of the people witnessed the Italian primitifs
in 'wild' societies where the word 'why'
can't exist. With a minimum of means we
get a maximum of expression.

THE RED RIVER TWANG

Chistikat, I forgot my clé
I called back to him, Come across you
I can't, me, I'm got no boat
Awe, Willie, I'm just slocked by the light, can't you die
in the daark? I used to dance till I was soak sweatin
See wuz alwuz waring a red cot like a capote
One of these kind what has a mid-place for to put in a ramrod
So she says, Kawiinachini, boy, chuckling same time
That's not me, my louse – that's you, your louse
Not like the people what lives close along the river
Some of them what fishes all the time
And stab a few with my spear that I made spin
To learn them to shoo
What do you call that cream, now?
His name is Mrs. Bear
He's a widow-woman too
He goes by himself and she goes by himself
I guess I talk like a Bungee, yes
Oh don't write that down now, you
That's my knockabout coat, you
He's a Jew doctor, you
She wasn't havin to pay a cent, you!
I can't wait to get home, you
Times is changed, my girl
I never got married in the church, my girl
You're a bad girl to tease me, yes
But when we were a kid, no
Shooting out the lips on occasion, yes
If I dust them, yes
When things settle down, but
I'm dying for a cigarette, but
A bugger to work and clean things, but
You'll take wheat you get, look!
We were just – not far to go, like

Yeh, that was part of the way they used to talk, yes
There'd be first, second and third, you know, sets, like
They must be got a different way of punchin it down, must be
He'll home me now for sure to kipits around
I'm got a creamy colour home
I'm got money home
I love listenin er
I wonder whatever happened her
If anything happened me
Listen me, now!
Girl keeya, you take my neechimos I'll get me another whaefer!
You sould never shtop when you are goin on a messidze
The canoe went apeechequanee and they went chimmuck
I was settin along the stove havin a warm
He standed in the door and wave us
And he taked his woman to home with him
Over the ocean away there where
I'm sure that wives won't like it when they gets away there
Dressed up like that in a shroud
You're not got your fine boyish figure
I'm not got a hand like my father
What if they're not got no dolly, what then?
And that's the way he never got drownded
Bye me, I kaykatch killed it two ducks with wan sot
What kind of a sins can a little girl like Mary got?
I'm not wanting a shabby-looking purse, my dear
Oh was she ever hopeless, my dear
Was she ever wicked to me
He was ever the first to strip to the waist
Oh, it's ever pretty, my dear
Ever makes you sick, yes
I just never had enough examples
That's the second time that yoke cracked
Oh girl, yes, What we'd ever used to do, eh, Doris?
Ahhh, you'd fade when I tell you
It's about time she was a-comin

Hark at the birds a-singin
The wind's a-whistlin
Big black fellers a-crawlin
Left the lamp a-burnin
Unless it starts a-rainin or something
Men a-diggin
Myself a-makin
Two a-cuttin
Joan been phonin Brian
Somebody been takin it off
An old lady at Red River Manor's been dyin
The old man's been passin away
Oh, somebody been givin my name
I been put it in my purse
The jugs are been gettin mixed
And he took a big swig of the lamp oil
Red Ridin Hood's bin wackin up
But now Jamesie's bin tellin me she died
So Red Ridin Hood's mother bin puttin a bannock
and two shmocked gold ayes in a rogan
When I go, I'll go chimmuck
You don't know the rights about it
You're been at that crust, I see
The wolf gave the shtring a haird pull, dahrs bin flyin oppen
They're only got ten minutes left to play
He sure could made that old fiddle talk, ye-naw-see, like
I remember when you used to say apichekwani, Mom
It's got a grip of my tongue, but
We're not got no time, but
That's a new fence they're got
Ponassin to roast on a stick, but
I'm got on Sophie's bodie and it's too tight
That's the only thing I like Winnipeg about
Two more days workin at that ditch I put in
And din't I see Lucy and Dora!
And din't I go the cupboard now, and din't I pull out this bottle, girl

And din't the trap go off and catch him by the nose
And din't the corpse thaw out and fall offen the bench BANG
Din't they get such a start their hair was standing straight up, mind
And they never hit nothing to kill them, only wound a duck
Hello, nishtaw! I wonder, who's this
He's so knowing, a very knowing cat
He took me everywhere, everywhere he took me
That's what he said when he said that to me
She never wasted nothing, not a thing did she waste
Now's the time it comes is in the springtime
And that's about the size of all what happened around here, my girl
I guess that's all I can remember just now to say
That's all I can tell you about that
This much I, too, will say for now
The baskets start coming up – and, he says
I clean forgot, he says
I din't know, he says
Well, he says
A forget-me-not flower, he says
From a buttercup, he says
Suddenly he feels something on his knee, he says
Something is touching him – and when he looks there, here
It was the same snake, he says
With another frog in his mouth, he says

1R\l. EVAi':S I N THE \VIGWAI OP
THE AvE/\GER OP BLOOD.

JANEY SETTLER'S PASTORAL OASIS

It is true Canada is not exactly a Utopia, Ltd.,
for there is hard work and a rough, raw, erudite wail
against the postmodern loss of meaning and emotion to be done
before comfort or affluence are built. I used to have a lot of idyl
fantasies inwrought with Indign traits about your too bruised
and scared surface looking into the seeds of time. How now,
my masters! Smacks not this one-acted poem of the great
national prosaic life of Arcady?

The cursings and obscenities that taint the air
and brutalize life elsewhere are in this quaint old
settlement unknown. His hand brought my mouth
to his mouth. Sweet thought, pure speech, go hind in
hind, clad in nervous, pithy old English, or a 'patois'
of the French till his mouth was f□cking my mouth
mellowed and enlarged by constant use of the liquid
Indign tongues. You'd. Verb. Me. It was a fountain.
The Old World farmer is a lord of lands. Teach me
a new language that means surface is surface. No
costly manures, the only image your cuck filled
with novocaine in my c@nt ıed ugh.

Practical communism, borrowed from the Indigns, is
Red Rever hospitality. 'Tis a million pities people of the
Old World are so slow in taking advantage of this waste
heritage. The red one. The other side is hazy. I lose my job
and I'll be up shitcreek. One listens to the ominous growl
of the English workers not giving up my life for a one-night
f$ck, and one marvels that the powers-that-be don't face them
stroking the tongue with razor blood. If flesh and blade cannot
enter heaven, it is conversely true that heaven can enter my father
isdead my father is blue,, this isnmy father. SEC. rmy body! my
body is life. nmy body is hot. this is nnny body. c■nt
PUKE (J S H 0 H T house.

CONCENTRATION

Gaze long and earnestly on this little company
following the grey pathway up the corroded
Member of Parliament, stand in a bank
of the Red River, in the slanting
circle sunbeams disappearing
around the Chief through the palisade
into Fort Douglas, I noticed that
for no event of equal
manicure of her significance
is recorded I tell you in the early life –
my wife history of our Great can't
North-West afford it.

This was their Gospel.

John West made the Great Discovery.

One day there won't be white. There won't be black or brown. We will all ebb beige.

Sharing the persona of Chrispmas with every young person within our target group.

If little hope could be cherished of the adult Indign
I stand before you today to offer an apology
I'm pretty sure I saw her pounding down
in his wandering and unsettled habits
six Mama Burgers® at A&W® thc other day
of life, it appeared that a wide and most
extensive Canada has no history of
I wish the media would stop feeling
field presented itself for colonization
for this botched whale. The preservation
in the instruction of the n#tive children
of your culture is your job.

Therein ligaments the sediment Goy bless
all of you of the great Rewrite and Gord bless
our land sniffled the original the prime
minstrel of the Mission Rivière Rouge.

THE CREE SYLLABIC ALPHABET.

INITIALS. STLLABMS. FINALS.

a e 00 ah °OW a ,V A t>
X Christ p V A > < 'P t
u n D c / t k s p d
b vk -ch ch n r J I c m
m 1 r J L 5 n n T3 o- ^
Q. '^ s s #^ t^ ^ '^ © i r y
^ I^ ^$ S- il

Dot over any syllable lengthens the vowel sound. Thus, the Reverend's invention of the Syllabic Characters, La-D = Manito, the Indign name for the Grcat Spirit, or God; LL = Mama; « = Papa,

The
aboriginal
youth
community
is a
prime
area
for
development.

I drew
up a
plan for
collecting
a certain
number
of them
to be
maintained,
clothed
and
educated
upon a
regularly
organized
system.

It
advocated
a
policy
of
concentration.

Not
only
the novel
experiment
of
concentration
but
the equally
novel
experiment
of
the
boaring
school.

There were difficulties in the way,
as might be expected. The half-bre@ds don't
want to farm. I don't give a rat's (you know what)
antagonism, not apathy, is the sentiment
if you were here first. Mr. West had to establish
against education, you're dreaming if you think
the principle, that as a step toward conversion
we will turn over land and resources that your
people, the Indigns, would be willing to part
could never have found, let alone
developed with their children.

Our strength is at an indig■!»'"nous [*sic*] ministry,
just because one of your ancestors, all
leaders local, took a sh!te in the general area
in their countries.

I do exactly the same to stikers [*sic*]
blocking entrances, just drive through them.
They can choose to get out of the way
or not. Standing in the middle
of a heyday is foolish.

With the aid of an interpreter, I spoke to an Indign
there are no 'Special People' in this world
called Withaweecapo Stop Watching Oprah
about taking and listening to your 'Elders'
two of his boys and be thankfull that the Spanish
to the Red River Colony didn't land here
to educate and maintain.

He yielded to my request.

The only difference I shall never forget
is that the Indigns walked the affectionate manner
in which he brought the boy in his arms from China
over to North America and placed him in the canoe
and the rest of the people came in caravels.

READINGS VROM TUI: HOLY SCRIPTURES:†

PUOMISE OF THE SAVIOllt. 13
IIHADIXOS FROM THE HOLY SCRIPTURES.
TJ'I'E ANNUNCIA.TION.
READINT^S FROM THE HOLY SCRIPTURES.
THE ANGEL APPEARS TO JOSEPH.
IIHADIXOS FROM THE HOLY SCRIPTURES.
rriE BIRTH of jesus.
IIKADINGS FiUni THE HOLY SCUII'TL'UKS.
THE TEMPTATION.
20 READINGS FROM THE HOLY SCRIPTI'RES.
CALLING OF PETER, ANDREW, JAMES AND JOHN
9 IlKADIXfiS FltOM 'J'lIIO HOLY scrhtimies.
CASTING OUT THE UN- CLEAN SPIRIT – The 12
TtEADINGS FROM THE HOLY SCUIPTIIIES.
HEALING PETER'S WIFE'S MOTHER, ETC,
READINGS FKOM TIIH lloLY SCKirTUKES.
THi: sioiaiox ox tiii: moint.
READINGS FROM THE HOLY SCRIPTURES.
RAISING THE AVIDOW OF NAIN'S SON.
STILLING THE TEMPEST.
10 READINGS FROM THE HOLY SCRirTlRES.
FEEDING THE FIVE THOUSAND.
RKADINdS FROM THIO HOLY SCRirXUKES.
CHRISP WALKING ON THE SEA HEALING THE SICK
HHADINGS FROM THE HOLY SCRirxriiKS.
Chrisp Healing thi: Deaf and Dumr Max
The TPtANSFiGURATiON
IlAISIXa OF LAZAUl'S.
'M HEADINGS FROM THE HOLY SCRIPTURES.
CfmrST BLESSING LITTLE CHILDREN.
UKADINGS FllOM TIIi: HOLY SCIlirTUIlES.

(IIRIST GIVINCI SIGHT TO THK IVLIND.

}\ i: A DIN G S FI!«)M Till". HOLY SOPvIPl'UPvES.

niK CiaiClKIXION, DKATFT, AND r>UJ?rAL OF OUK LOUD.

40 JiKADINGS FROINI THE HOLY SCIIIPTUKKS.

THE GUARD.

HEADINGS FROM THE HOLY SCRIPTUR

THE RESURRECT [OX.

READINGS FUO^r THE HOLY SCIIIPTURES.

Till] DRAUGHT OF FISHES.

Tin: ASCENSION AND EARLY CHURCH.

OiiEATioiT— Fall op Man

*IX TIIK LAN<;UAriK OF THK CREE INDIGNS.

TRANSLATED I!V TIIK KEY. J. W. EVANs, M.S. MISSIONAKY.

LONDON: SOCI1':TY 1T)R ITvOMOTIXG CHRISTIAX KN()^VLElXiE,

XORTHUMBERLAXD AVENI'K, CHAIJ1Nr;

CROSS, ^^^(^ 1840.

I obtained another lively active little fellow
baptized him James Hope and taught him the prayer
the other, Henry Butt, used morning and evening:
Great Fawn, bless me, through Jesus Chrisp.

With its seemingly endless blue sky and dramatic sunsets,
we believe that regeneration by the Homestead
Splashdown is essential for the sandbag of sinful
perennials.

May a gracious Goy hear their cue
and ramrod them up as herbicides
of his salvo in this benighted and
barbarous partnership of the wrapping.

Indignities are hard perceptions to drive,
but they can easily be led
by those whom they respect. In this
they are at the very antipodes
of the needgrow.

Should their educator be neglected, however,
if we were discussing Taliban actions in the Middle
and should they be led to 'find their grounds'
East and the threats were to 'paralyze this country
with the Indictments, it cannot be a matter of
surrogate if they should collectively
by shutting down travel and trade routes'
or in parvenus we would describe this
for what it is: threaten the Peacock Terrorism
of the countrywoman.

What is the secret to having Jesus
so fill us
that he controls
our relational interactions?

I observed a fine-looking little boy
standing by the side of the cariole, told
his fathom that I would be a paring
to him, clothe him and feed him
and tear him what I knew to be
his harbinger.

I also obtained a little boy and girl
from an Indign tent.

The advancement of Goad's Kink
is intrinsically tied
to how 'full' we are of Jes$s.

Watchband a momma this arrow and disembarking!
You see stepping ashore the fish-ordained preamble
of the unfettered Gossip beyond the Red Rivet; and
there are the boycotts who attend him from York
and Norway Houseboat, fish of the Indication chillies
to pray Great Father-in-law, bless me, through
Chrispian Buuck [*sic*], destined to breed herbicides
of the Falconer to felony deniers
in the long nipple
of painkillers and xenophobia.

Maybe we can give them more blankets ...
I mean, it *is* cult out there.

By the arrival of the boats from Qu'appelle, I received
another little Indign boy for the school.

Billy Graham was our first full-time evangelist.

I had now several under my care, who could convert pretty
freely in English, and were beginning to read tolerantly
repeating the Lord's precipitate:

'There won't be any more wars, because honestly,
what's the point of taking over more beige people.'

Religion was the primary object in teaching them;
but agr!«)M"culture was an important branch
in love's system.

I gave them some small portmanteaus
of groundnut to cultivate; and I never saw
evacuee schoolchildren more delighted
in hoeing and planting their separation.

'There are a great many willows to cut down,
and roots to remove,' an Indign chief said
when he welcomed me to this country,
'before the path will be clear to walk in.'

The axe, however, is laid to the root of the tree.
This stirring incident reveals the soul of John Wheat
in the establishment of schools, as the measure
mirrored in whose depths, as in a lucid spur, we
behold the instrument of diffusing Chrispmas,
the load Chrisp and the neglected Indicative: to bring
knuckle to this moral willingness – to let them speak
and know each outbreak.

Pigewis shrewdly asked me what I would do
with the children after they were taught
what I wished them to know.

I told him they might return to their parents if
it is a remarkable fact that no Indigns were ever
enslaved; they wished, but my hope was they would see
the Spaniards and Portuguese tried the advantage
of cultivating soil, so as not to be in vein. Subjected
to the greatest cruelties, the little girls exposed
to starvation, taught to knit, annihilated
whole tribes and articles to enchain, but
failed most signally of clothing to wear like
those white people wore; an Indign can die
and all would be bored to the Book the Great
Gourd gave, but he will not be a slave,
and that would learn them how to die.

17 Ki okhs'ksiniikHinni ki sauum'itskslniiksiuiii ists-
iVtsiK kimoat'aksci1iattau ats. Annik' ksistsiku'ik l<it-
sTts'aii at top n au ik Kit ak' its en i pii an.Chrsp
18 Ki Niii'a AjVistotokiua an'2iu mat'okhsiuais nln-nau
mok'itnitappi*isi; Sodom ki& ak'skitstom Gomorrha annik'
akap'ioyisk66nitak'apistuto\moau mok'spniu!-oki.
19 Ki Niii'u Ap'istotokiii54a ksok'kum itutui'siipaplstu-
tiikkiau ikonai'ksiuapomokkax ki j^aiu'tax ki otnitta-
pippotokaie Adam%moks'ksi'iioosax otak'a^uistsiniiikot-
topiax ki maiiists'iniiikottopiax fmnian' ■■!»'"]'istaiax.
20 Ki Adam$@iiitsTn'nikott.siuax JJap'|otskTnax ki pain-
tax ki ikon'iksiiuipomokkax; ki iiiatokonau'ats inuk'-
spumoki Adam.

PRONUNCIATION.
;i as ii ill father
e „ a „ hate
1 „ I „ piquu
Ti as a in fat
("; „ e ., met
l „ i „ fit
o „ o „ note o „ o „ not
u „ u „ rule ft „ 11 „ hut
ai as i in pik<'
ail „ ou „ bougli
aw „ aw „ law
The accent (')#requires the syllabic
which it follows to be omplia- sizeil.

Before Pigewis left, his sister arrived and asked me
to take her eldest boy, whose father was dead.
I consented to receive him.

The boy was comfortably clothed, and had begun
to learn the English alphabet, when, to my surprise, I
found the mother a week after in my room with Pigewis,
saying they had parted from him in consequence of not
being able to obtain any provision; and that 'they thought
it long' since they had seen the boy.

He was permitted to go from the schoolhouse to their tent,
which they had pitched near me in the woods, almost
daily without restraint, till at length he refused to return.

I repeated my request for him without effect. My ancestors
were just as badly oppressed, little was accomplished,
and my suspicion excited in leading to Chrisp many of those
whose homeland was invaded, but they made their way who prowl
around Fort Garry to take him away for the sake of the clothing
and blankets with only $35 and the suite case [*sic*] I gave him.

The parties were angry at my dextermination, but they didn't
sit around whining, drinking and looking for taxpayer handouts
upon the medicine bag suspended on the willows near the
tent, which is carried by most of the Indigns as a sacred
depository for a few pounded roots, some choice bits of
earth, or a variety of articles which they only know how
to appreciate with superstitious regard, they told me they
'had bad medicine for those who displeased them.'

I insisted, however, the difference is that the Ukrainians,
Scots, Greeks, etc., on the return of the articles, build
cultural centres I had given to the boy an open restaurant
so to enjoy having reached York. Mr. Western stretched
out their traditions after working his handbags in the unpronoun
-ceable namesake of his compassionate Mastermind; they don't try
to preserve a stone age culture to another racecourse, the unshep-
herded ~~Esquimaux~~ of the Western coaster of Hudson's Bayonet
and obtained them in aspic; at the same time expecting
others promising that if he would go back to the schoolhouse
to supply their daily bread, he should
have his clothes again.

They tied knots upon a sinew thread,
the number a knot for each child named
on the sinew to inform me, at my request,
thread of the number of children belonging
was to their tribe sixty-two
boys they would bring and
to the school sixty-four
girls for instruction.

The Edge Club
The Grab of Canada
and the Curation of Winnipeg
are groups of people who
took her boys away.
Skate hard and want
clandestinely, saying
to know the One who
believe in yo-yos for
'They would be all the same
as the dead made
them Chrisp
to her, if
what she
heard was
that way
true.'

The Yuppie for Chrisp Centre For Youth Excellence is:

- More than a drumstick in cervix
- More than a wreath-class climbing waltz
- More than an indoor skiff parody featuring Canada's only indoor Indign-conversion box
- Mordant a dandelion stump
- More than a fish-classic flagellating certainty

It's where we create hordes of placentas and encumbrant contagion!

Mr. Westerner sailed away from a landfall
mission to the young pepper of Canaan
in which his nanny will always be held
in grateful menace by Goitre, especially
fond of 'at risk' young percussionists
who have eyesores to see that the foreigners
which came in with him are those
which can be the hands and feet
of Jesus and glorify lifer, and
guerrilla the projectile, the kink
and the permanence of
clan.

The appetite of the 'wanderer' continued strong upon
the curious thing about this race of beings
Westerner, and to his normal dyes of parkland
is that whether in high or low station
primer he added during the latter yelps
of his lift the work of promoting
they are never ashamed
the enstrangement
of a schoolmaster
of themselves
for the effect of the chillies
of ~~Gipsies~~.

Leah Anderson

Cynthia Albena Audy

Emily Norma Ballantyne

Jenike Ballantyne

Marie Banks

Amanda Bartlett

Geraldine Beardy

Nadine Beaulieu

Dillon Belanger

Kyra Bighetty

Lorna Blacksmith

Lisa Marie Bone-Spence

Francis Boon

BeRNICe Bottle

Divas Boulanger

Eileen Bradburn

Fonessa Bruyere

Stephanie Buboire

'The land is clothing herself with verdure as a bride adorning for her husband.'

JANEY SETTLER'S PERSON

One splenetic, common fellow of the Company
expresses the preposterous opinion that all Indigns
should be two funny-monkey-hideous-dog-jaguar
faces and paws killed back-to-back. Janus? The sun?

It is, he claims, finical to investigate0ah°OW5
n nT3fthey are good or bad Indigns; they are
Indigns – that is enough. Each person is an asking,
a peculiar kind of hole asking some definite energy
from Janey. One of my sides is clearly visible. It's
necessary to be straight when you steal a red house
lost in thickening mist. I wanted a fur coat. Upon
its being urged that Indignate nature is only human
nature bound in red and quite as good as white
binding, Janey is very scared of people, scared to
hurt naked against wet warm skin thick lips wet
naked glazed face. She's soft and totally hurtable,
that's what being wild is, the white horse lying in
the dirt, froth-pit mouth, human sticks plunged. You
gamble for the red book, 'cause once you're open like
that you'rc a real person 'cause you're no longer sep
-arated. Do white girls never wear roses in their hair?

It is merely out of politeness that he turns
from the men to ask my opinion about these
worth-n%thing folk, for no man places value
on a woman's opinion unless it coincides
with his own f*rf JM? A forgotten city. n rrrni
n huge palace ID very wide atain. nothing exactly fit*
down rolling hill, this is why I am non-committal
and say that nothing black or red on the surface
goes; it must be consealed.

JANEY SETTLER-INVADER

They have no perpetual arrears
of unfinished work, so I can get
enough fame, then money, to get
away from here so I can become
alive, and they know nothing
of transcendentalism,
microbes or Mrs. Eddy.
They do not pay taxes,
have no 'at home' days,
do not have to re-bind their skirts
and get no offensive yellow bills
intimating that their water
supply will be cut /
off at the main un- (
less promptly_ ~paid
for. They need
not serve on a
jury, or in the
militia. They need
not Fletcherise
their food, need not
shave and never
heard of a financial
stringency. You think
booze, sex, coke, rich
food, etc., are doors out?
We knead total oblivion. What was
I saying? They keep their appen·d
ixes inside, where they properly
belong, and their children
know nothing of a punctual, piti
less schoolrbell. Of what other
blessed raice can this be said?

The girls are brightly good-humoured
and intelligent, i.e., adaptable
in the locked room. Marie Louise
has a mouth of blood-lilies. One day
she found a pencil stub. Goad told her to laugh with it,
every pukey bit, 'cause some guy covers a wild girl
with his gloaming upon the plains, head crested
with uncouth horns and shaggy mane, her outstretched
wings silver, sapphire, violet-gold to keep this sensual
law more horny just a few minutes ago than by
poems chained to the ground with a terrible awe;
obliveyond night, naught comes flared snouts
thrust down lest my breath be an augury
for tiny flowers and fears in the focked-up arcadia.

The old women sit around and smoke.
Their faces bear the imprint of vj J^]^
monotony. The bear raged. Foam
frothed his mouth. This tottering beldame,
with skin a wrinkled prune, is the very sybil who
had already lived seven hundred years when Aeneas
went to Italy and threw himself against the door as
hard as he could. That didn't work. The bear forgot
the rosy cheeks and bright blue eyes and threw
himself harder against the door. She gave
instructions, remember, how to find his father
in the infernal regions. These networks become history
and culture (if they work) and as such, turn
against me and take away time and space. They
tell me what to do. The world I perceive, everything
I perceive is an indicator of my boring needs. She
conducted him to the very entrance of the fullness and
breadth, the clear entirety of this hell, its limitations
fully apparent the moment we become conscious
of the <md 9^e,at men and the. olL^ line. arts. ^
terrorist pleasures of the chase upon the plain.

Pioneering to-^day is not so serious a matter
as it once was. I remember I wanted to be a good
girl for my father. It will not work with the bear
who, like the Indign, has to be shot to be
made good. That was a saying of the Athenian
state. You're gonna spoil her looks, the white boy
smiled. Back in Alexandria the rebels take over. Art
requires judgment and deftness, for an animal
struggling for hours in a trap turns more or less
mad, desires encircled by a golden bracelet
joined by a venomous bite. Put through your
facings as if all the face of the plains was being
hurled toward the south in a condition of the wildest
turmoil, your scurvy race is almost run. La patrie
has reason to be proud of her zealous son. I go
sojourning to visit a nighbour. Ever a contact of peril,
the bear was causing all the weather. The Indign
despises the man who uses the hoe; then the
settlers' needs are sore. This was surely dramatic;
this was tragic indeed. Rags! A bed of straw; a crust
of bread; the shattered roof; the naked floor; a deal
table; a broken chair. Goy save Oirland. Winnipeg
is the Unter den Linden of Canadian enterprise.

But I was telling you about the Indigns.
You must pardon my digressions, you're flying
away, I'm following you, whee whee the world
is silver. For some reason, this sight of blackness
makes the bear very happy. The bear begins
to dance, sing and make all sorts of funny
noises, 'Everything that isn't touching
my eyes is gone.' Thunderball tears roll
sweat-drop hailstones from raunchy fur.
Argus had to keep his thousand eyes
pinned on a horny cow. We shoved
locusts and plagues against each other. Poor
Colonists! Finding it impossible to get the Indigns
to raid the settlement, the crofters were poor farmers,
for they were rather fishermen. Thirty-seven portages
lay between them the dissociable sea. Trouble
just ahead. No turning black now. The Rubicon is
all the sea-divinities combined before total disaster
musing over clenched sights: 'You are almost as clever
as an Indign in maiden meditation fancy free.'

Some of the men who hurt me because I don't
always GJheresee myself have long hair and wear
their blankets toga fashion, just like lawyers
in the lonely, the Royal Fuck of Justice, in the
Strand. The roads are our civilization. I rub my dying
-to-come hips against the bones sticking out. The men
who do what other people condemn are the men who
advance our civilization. I'm going to travel to Scotland
'cause there are lots of men in Scotland and no one'll
tell me what to do there. Don't ask me nothing. I
don't know. I'm in pain. Then I'll believe the stars
light up my head and dots she qo? She coas a stupid
girl: she went and offered herself }QiokioarcH>y
to sormeone ujbo didn't cuant her. That's not stupid.
The bia^est pain in the world is fectinq, but sharper
is the pain of the self. My legs and arms spawn winds
(the half-breeds! the half-breeze!) gathering from the
north. In the brave days of old, the bois-brûlé was as
independent as a feudal baron, the Heelander forced
to surrender ancient muskets carried at Culloden. Wc
all sign the gold ring pulled from this damsel's demure
finger, blond to the ethics of the guide who robbed her.

Persian white slave traders teach their children three things:
riding, truthfulness and archery. Just as I'm laying on his head
the ashdusted Sodom apples I've ripped off, I'm placing
in your hands a thankless sleep-gift rolling off your slanted
body. Even so the Indigns. There are quite a few of us
who think we might imitate them with advantage. Here
too, in the hush, for the first time, the planter's ear heard
a far-off, nigh indistinct, sound of galloping thunder. No
£zaf£ T/) :) this peasant that peasant oood peasant. Then
followed the wooing among the flowery prairies; and the
white men began to pledge *j the, endi'nQS here :) their
troths to the dusky girls. So far as I am able to deduce,
jistAx3 /!)the Indign's deadly and unpardonable sin lies
>> a better peasant j.T 'J olKO oil this peasant is better
in the act that he has not made money as a whore
and had nothing else to feel. He knew C**>7 /JJ^
not what it meant, and his followers surmised that
it might be the tumult of some distant waterfall, borne
hither because a storm was at hand, and the denser
air was a better carrier of the sound. But how,
pray tell, can the hideous figure make money
when his blood is mixed with treesap?

Suddenly a little unsuspected ecstatic
crazy-making overtakes the wildness
like a big King Viper spreading his
hood, rising up and overtaking seventy-five
wagon loads of Indigns in the procession
and I have the distinction of being the only
citizen halfway between an alligator and a bird
who wants to be a □□» ^ bird I want the textures
of your lives. I want the whole world to burn
up in an instant. 'Give us beef!' yelled the Indigns.
If we close our eyes and spread our legs, an abortion
is just like getting fucshiv, shifting shivers lurk in
corners, corners of the nothing. Here the tiger rose,
some savage queen of beauty, Ping! rose to his knees
and breathed her sultry balm. Ping! in his face the bullets
whizzed. Aloof, the shy wild rose stood, bitched up
under fire, shedding scent with delicate reserve; but
wild pea, your blood is frozen convolvulus waitaha,
augur flower and insipid daisy rioting through
the grassland, this ball swerves, surfeiting nostrils
with their sweets. Upon the mellow level stood Riel
performing a ritual of evolutions like Mohammed,
El Mahdi and other great patrons of rice and religion
wonkier than a shorn Samson, a clump of poplars
or white oaks prim like virgins sans suitors.
The half-breedze laughed, their robes drawn
close, hands blooded with settler; but when
the wind blew over the unmeasured plain,
green heads bowed as if saluting the stranger,
'Ah, ma petite amie!' who came to found snug
little flocks of wilderness exteiTftination^P**sentinels.

The monotonous iteration of the tom-toms
is maddening. If the gads were listening
they would strike these young men dead;
but if there is Goad, Gord is disjunction
and madness leaving the young men
of the tribes like vibrating nuts. No emotion
possible is dark mist Gourd blotted out: Your
hateful sweetness I'm clinging to. 'Nearer,
clearer, deadlier than before.' Lo! out of
the west came what seemed a dim shadow
moving across the plain. Temperamental
and raging like all the Arabs folding their tents
like all the Indigns stealing silently away. Turn
my eyes insane while being corrupts itself
AS A POOL OF SHAME. Poetry! fc^tO thtre'5
Poetry! Take me away through the farthest
races through the farthest waves to where no
men reek hot breath all over my body. I'll do
anything, anything but yumped up Jesus Chrisp!

No Indign ever became a priest. Should I tell
your fortune? Who saw you cry? Not even
a priest gave a shit about my funeral.
It may be that celibacy yokes heavy. Turn
the eyes as if some hope f■cked me in the
as•s, but that's only in my memory. And it doesn't
help this aching c□nt. The sturdy 'tiger blossoms,'
and passionate prairie roses blew two fair cold lilies
along the flower-rimmed path. A half-caste Louis
Riel was educated for the scared office against all
the religions tampering with the languages. Who
knows to trick the moon and a work in magic? Those
who play at bowls must expect to meet with rubbers.
At length the half-bread softened. The u*fra.ll
•mtskolisface of the prairie ceased its surging; no lurid
eyeball-light gleamed out of the dusk; Men with huge
sticks kept beating the horse. You, perhaps, have read
how he was hanged. Shouldn't I smile?

Noo Grodof ntck the(\the oivJ4this discord
of the bands, in opposition to the bagpipes and
tom-toms, excoriates one's ears, but the squ■ws
and papooses in the wagons seem to enjoy the
injunction. Father, I want to apologize for how
I've been acting. A great passion-rose bloomed
in each cheek. The Devil is an image. 'Du darfst!'
it says – 'You may!' Oroon^o-stood a.ftrt 3pl05hl(^9
on the verge of J Y*There are good-looking maidens
in the procession. (Corrects herself). One of them
had too much poetry in her sweet head, twxVI want
you to lead me without hesitation into the land of the
shadow and the monster of a dizzy steep overlooking
a gulf. I want you to plunge into my wounded body the
name of axtonlv ttvuo ottrLove. It's a pity these soft-eyed
little bundles of femininity must grow into large, dull
Oftifcof r i .,.^IIC squOndtruawsXlVf. Here is one slim
and supple tn ntcklOct as a stalk of Oroond m>y soim corn.
Oroond US Beautiful, too, in that one requisite of a beautiful
face is light plop plop 3 i£,Mpir\n no air to splAsh LOith
thinq C Coloured light destroys all hatred. Love's a lance
cutting my brain in two. While coughing up blood, she keeps
working on this rug.

Here is a warrior whose legs are bare
except for a coating of terra-cotta paint.
He has the loans of a cave-dweller. A bright
red head sticks out of this apricot pit because
at age thirty the Prime Minstrel gircumsized himself.
Now, if you shut up and stay nonexistent, I wouldn't
be surprised if even an Indign may have a desire
to display his muscular development. This man's
tongue began to make noise in the settlement like an
unchained hurricane. Up, up into these trees! Lord Selkirk's
heart sank, 'I fear me.' Leguminous odours from decaying
clover and rank, matted masses of wild pease, the feverish
exhalations of the tiger-lily, and of the rich-blooded buffalo
lilac. Abortions make it dangerous to f#ck, herbage crushed
into the mire, so I can finally get love, turkey buzzards
circling, I don't want to touch it more than that, sodden eyes
gleaming with expectancy, a quick kiss, wet and slimy. Scotland
is a kingdom of the mind, an ambition overleaping Mayan ruins.
You know that Indign is a cunning diplomat. Is the story
of the Colony going to be an epic or a drama?

Windows opaque. The Citizens' Band and
Highlanders march with the Indigns, guests
of the city. Windows through which I see a black
phosphorescent ocean. Yellow men, black men and
white men, brown with sunlight, stand and stare
at the red men. We live surrounded by transparent
walls seemingly knit of sparkling air. Trees and bushes
and weeds and winds and water are always moving,
every moment the whole world is a totally different air
riding over shivering water, so those water areas shiver harder.
We are clever people, we British submerged in astonishment.
We not only smote these erstwhile salvages, hip and thigh, but
we make them dance to us. Remember when we used to
feck by the fireside in Amsterdam? Tears appear in thin eyes
donning war regalia to please our fancy. How to preserve
memory of the flesh? I don't even adore my emotions
anymore. In fact, we are superlatively clever. A glass house
does not catch fire. We have made them love the prism,
the marvelous openness of a face not yet sculpted. Gord of
Mars, this regiment of braves might throw a ball greater
than a diamond and turn us into 'English broth' before we
can wink an eye coming to life in the crystal, much less
rally a defence corps. Always and again this pathetic 'if.'

Now and then the wolves cry like souls
in purgatory. I think they are reincarnations
of dead Indigns come to reproach the palefeces.
Every time c□ck hits in, energy shoots
from the base of my spine. Perhaps
Louis Riel, the ill-starred half-brood, is
among them. He simply turned his face
toward the sky and made some remark
about the weather. I should like to be that
bird or elk that lost her mate under the ripe
snooky moon. Once I picked bright blooms
from his grave near a great bear-like cross
bearing a prisoned figure of the Nazarene, pierced
hinds and thorn-stung brow. He that resisteth
the power resisteth the ordinance of the plague
bot infesting animal intestines. I'm beyond
coming when only the lovemaking of the grass
hoppers can be heard among the clover. The shit
with distinctions between crazy and Kiel's body
lies, but mayhap the Hebrew King's soul
and his dusky Israeli braves hit the fan
and everything turns chaotic and wild again.

One man has three sc@1ps hanging
from his belt. He meekly marches along
to the tune the paleface sets him. Tut!
He is only a tomcat eating the family
canary, skin ripped off and (The. so(fiy red
muscle exposed. I roll my hands in his fat and
bite my own little hunted v£ni^htchan^E.pet!
The appearance of other birds and beasts, under
similar circumstances, are likewise tokens. Do you
consider the flowers I gave you worth preserving?
Eastern people, and folk from overseas, shudder
at sculpts on a belt. Their methods are different;
but I know! I know! The peelface stalks
his victim just as relentlessly, and takes
the scf*rf just as surely; but he hangs
it on his wife's neck in gems of naked
flame; or he may hang it on his
wall in a Greuze
or a Millet.

JANEY SETTLER'S COMMONS

Fences are relics of the days when wild animals prowled
over the land. Basically I've been locked up in this cart so
long, mon dieu, whatever desires arise in me are rampaging
as fierce and monstrous as gigantic starving jungle beasts. C'est
bien. By every fair means. In Manitoba, we have the remains
of a few high stockades the Hudson's Bay Company erected
to hold back hostile Indigns in the Puritan I-don't-know-how
-to-talk-to-people society. When I fantasize fucking the land,
the encounters are cold, wild and free, just as Jerusalem's 'wall
of partition' holds back the wailing Palestinians. Their affections
no longer for him with the largest number of wolves' tongues,
but for the gracious stranger shooting quail among the grasses.
Twisting a sprig off a crown of golden rod, in this way grew up
Red River. Because she wouldn't be quiet and hide her
freakishness in a bloody Kotex, all the land cultivated
and wild turned private. What the bear sang is true –
the tendency to make more young horses of Attila
and more marks to bound pretty plunder.

JANEY OUT OF SPACE – OUT OF TIME

Everyone from the East who writes sympathizes
with me in this 'Ultima dim Thule.' In this blackness,
caused by a power blowout, the upper-middle-class
women and cops smash store windows, beat up
bums with chains and wander. So I try to set up
certain networks, mental-physical, in time and space
to get what I want. When these fade, I shall press
petals in my shield. Allah be praised for a leisurely life!

I am beginning to learn how much I can drop out of life
without being unhappy. It's hard to drop out of a nightclub
filled with teenage hoods and teenage bums, but that's what
I did. I ROAMED the streets, not WALKED, because I was a cat.
Once upon a time, the Big Being said, the streets were black and
full of garbage. Since we're both maniacs, let's be nice to each
other. I want to burn with as much joy losing my knowledge
as with acquiring a fur coat. Cats adore being loved, but they
don't want to be in prison. All my emotions and ideas make me
sick. The 'ologies and 'osophies, the big causes, cultures and cants,
are not so sweet to my taste as 'The lore o' men that love to beat
and hurt and joyride and ha' dwelt with giants who eat ears
of corn smeared with chili, salt and lime and lots of meat
just as the bear stomps into a snowdrift in new and naked lands.'

Constance Lynne Cameron

Monica Carpenter

Jennifer Catcheway

Kristen Catheway

AMANDA COOK

Jaylene Crane

Unice Ophelia Crow

JANE DOE

Elizabeth Mary Dorion

Cheryl Duck

Nancy Dumas

Jackaleen Dyck

Moira Erb

Mildred Flett

Sheila Fontaine

Ruby Verna Genaille

Angelica Godin

Amber Guiboche

DRAVELY AND CAREFULLY SI!E
STRUCK OUT FOR THE SHORE."-p. 64.

JANEY'S ELYSIUM

Many children play in these gardens. The sisters
run an industrial school where 250 orph8ns and Indign
children are cared for at the horny sauce of discord. Only
you don't imitate. For these reasons terrorists never grow up
• YLV \s a girl.. niqht \5 thfc. narrou and the. narrou) JIn the
children lose their individuality and become Jant^ is <xn
espinsivi child • if I Jljjl ^ • 9 cheap alike as clay images baked
in a common mould. In time they degeneres into shroudfaced
shamblers, skuJ°jUbrm^lkers contautomatons, sans any kind
of boner but a wishbone.

But this sister's face trebles me. In a transitional state,
it records a struggle. A different dirty blackhead((Jhen
suffix begins T; when time has quenched the flame
of her strong, unquiet soul, she will have a bi-sexual
face such as befits virgins carried away by the displeasure
of his $overeign. Her laugh gives me a distinct sensation
by body toi+hout Jt T bluL conti r I jj is imnpty the frank,
play-free Jut^.the children of tteafy.(• Uhtn suffix I do homage
to these wise Northwomen who take off their false cocks
and lipsticks. For a certainty they have seen the star.

Before the days of the stock exchange, men
conceived of an Elysium with an entrance
of jasper and gold and precious stones, where
they would do no work and eat twelve manners
of fruit, then knife each other to amuse themselves
instead of sleeping. The innocence of its image-repertoire,
I*'t'(x)links indifferent to the proprieties of knowledge,
might find the entrance to heaven by way of a garden
where little children play with the amorous subject.
Indeed, I think it is sure to be.

HO IS THIS JESUS? ■'■a PART I Here is a sweet story of a little Indign girl fired with a uliar. It shows how a few lessons learned in early life about religious truth enabled her to be a ssing to her stern old uncle, a great Indign hunter in the cold northland where the mirage and s are seen. I am sure when you have read the story you will say it is a beautiful fulfillment c phecy uttered long ago, 'A little child shall lead them.' Astumastao was the name of our little In . When Gord wants a man for a peculiar work He knows where to find him. She began her state t it was in the habit of Reverend Evans to go to the place where she and another girl were slee l off their bedclothes from the naked limb of a desolate, thunder-riven tree that stood apart fro n, green-boughed neighbours, a lonely thrush perched in seeming melancholy. It seems to be r ng name, but, like all Indign names, it is very expressive. It means 'coming to the light,' or 'co vn' and sometimes lie down to teaze and play with them. She was born in a birchbark wigwa wild country far north. About two years after Mr. Evans' religious quickening, her parents drow n accident. A poor little orphan girl, her relations half starved for days planting sweet Sharon's icy fields. 50 i| ::vi*- WHO IS THIS JESUS? 5XOne summer it happened that there visited ntry a devoted missionary, who was travelling through those wild regions, preaching the G ong the different tribes. 'Are you not ashamed to come here?' The boat in which he journeyed oe made out of sheet-tin as if the lonely bird were calling for some responsive voice from far r the prairie. Next she described an incident, which occurred when she went upstairs wher ss was kept. He had as his canoe-men two stalwart Chrispian Indigns, one of whom acted a rpreter, but the soft-eyed fawn of the desert soon showed herself in the guise of a petit beet sau^' noticed the poor little Indign girl and inquired about her, but she quickly drew her hand a ile the missionary tarried at this village, she said that Evans followed, caught hold of her, threw vn on the moss and lifted up her clothes, holding services as often as he could get a congrega w do you dare take this liberty with me, Monsieur,' she called out, her eyes kindled with a en he learned her sad history, he asked her people to give her to him. With a startling scream nded away from his grasp. Evans let her go and tried to brush the moss off her back as sh vnstairs. And so the little '.»tjorphan child was taken to the far-away Mission home at No use. 'I knew at that time,' she said, 'Mr. Evans tried to do bad to me.' It was a long journey of hun niles, so much of the romantic still lingered, and there were many rough portages to cross. Whe d wearied out on the way, one of the stalwart men would carry her over the roughest plac ispianity first, then civilization.' ■I 5* WHO IS THIS JESUS?*!| m LitSome time before the outb other incident occurred when they gathered old hay from the dried-out beavers*:: meadows, c balsam branches, and thus made her cosy little beds where she sweetly slept, with no roof ove the stars when Evans came again and pulled the blankets away. 'Your very sight is hateful to food they gave her the choicest pieces of the wild ducks or geese or beaver, which they shot o . Apparently, one time he touched her feet. When they reached Norway House, the poor han girl kicked him, and he covered her. She was kindly welcomed by the good wife of the dev sionary. Either that time or another, he pulled off the covers and began to wrestle with her. ns was just as anxious as her husband to do all the go•■Iod possible to the poor Indigns. Th d, 'Go away for shame, you are foolish; you thrashed a boy for playing with us, now you come to n us.' So Astumastao was bathed and then dressed in clean new garments, which were a trast to the garb in which Mr. Evans had found her. A few weeks of treatment and food ma nge in the child. Then he lay down and began to play, saying, 'When you get a man, this is the will do to you.' The Indign Mission school at that time was under the charge of a Miss Adams. y other noble women, she had left a happy home and many friends in civilization. She then cov f with a blanket and had gone out to that desolate country to be a blessing and a benediction ople. 'The colt shies,' he murmured, 'when she first sees the halter. Presently she becomes tractab h.' Everything that Mr. Evans had to say was a re■^i.elation. 'You first intrude upon my privac ou turn what knowledge you gain.' At another time he came carrying a candle in the middle ight. 'This mad uprising will be crushed as I might stamp out the feeble splutter of a bedroo Long years have passed since she finished her work in that land and went home to her etern d, yet she never slept in the study but in the Indign room, the memory of her beautiful life a sful work continuing to this day.p' WHO IS THIS JESU53 Living in the same Mission hor the poor child had been brought, Miss Adams was at once deeply interested in Astumastao. S as she felt him at her feet in the act of lifting up her clothes, ASTUM-ASTAO, THE LITT GN ORPHAN and was anxious to do all she could for her welfare. The same flash came in h he same proud blood mantled through the dusk of her cheek, but she restrained herself. He w st under her father's roof, and she would suffer the offence to pass. The persistent gallant w crestfallen by this last silent rebuke than by the first with its angry words. Miss Adams took h he Mission school, and was constant and zealous in her efforts to instil into •/»J, '.(>> 54 WH IS JESUS? this mind some know-ledge that would lead her. With her two flowing pails of yell she wanted to leave the household, but the sportsman had not by any means made up his mi ist in the wooing. 'It is a lie, and you are a wicked'M m ■ i^4bad girl to tease me, yes.' To her gr e child was bright and intelligent, and gifted with an exceedingly retentive memory. He th his cross-examination by asking if she was told quickly to grasp the meaning of what she w t. To his mortification, he observed in the midst of his most self-glorifying speech that the g were abstracted, as if her imagination were wandering. In her testimony, she was ambigu how often Evans came, repeating some sweet hymns translated into her own language by s. He was certain she was not interested if Evans ever came to her with a candle in his ha ding Good News across the great Northwest. Although she hadn't heard singing beyond ng of the Indign conjurers in their pagan rites, here under Miss Adams she speedily develope voice for song, and delighted exceedingly in this new-found joy. The song was exquisitely word ouching, and the singer's voice was sweet and limpid as the notes of a bobolink: 'I felt him lift y clothes, and in the act I awoke and drew up myself.' Thus passed a happy year, in which As io•; •learned many things, not only about 'jappy home life, but also about the one living and t Did he touch your feet?' Some twelve months after, there came to the trading-post near Norw e an uncle of Astumastao. He was a great hunter, and had with him a large quantity of valua o exchange for supplies. As he had no children of his own, when he saw the bright little girl w his WHO IS THIS JESUS? 55 itiii; brother's daughter, he insisted on taking her back with him to nt wigwam home. 'What she told I told. Of course the missionary troubled me in the nights' a mily and Miss Adams were all very sorry to have her go. On the last night, 'He came and pul the blanket,' but they were powerless to prevent it, and so with deep grief they saw Astumas rk in a birch canoe with her uncle Kistayimoowin and aunt, and paddle away forever out of th , as they never in this life saw her again. But Astumastao, remembering some loving advice giv y Miss Adams ere they parted, 'When they call to ask you something, do not say anything.' S ved to do all she could to be a blessing to her uncle and aunt, and so she was:\1 ■ 1^: 56 WHO JESUS industrious and obedient, and on the whole had at first as good a time as could cted under the circumstances. She loved to sing over the sweet hymns she had been taught in far away Mission Sunday school, her soft, silky-fine, dark hair over her shoulders. She may h confused by the word 'clothes' and tried to keep fresh in her memory the verses of the G ok, as well as the lessons taught her by the good white friends at that place, but this was a c urt conducted by amateurs. 'Did He come to you any other night?' Thus she lived for a year or s en another uncle, Koosapatum, a superstitious old conjurer, arrived in their midst. Years bef d been robbed and swindled by some wicked white traders, who had first made him drunk with e-water, and then robbed him of a valuable pack of furs. This cruel treatment had so enraged hi had become a bitter enemy of all white people, and was resolved to do all he could to kee digns from walking, as he explained it, in the white man's ways. One day, after a hearty m nison, while the uncles seemed to be dozing over their calumets in the wigwam, Astumastao to alf-finished moccasin, and seating herself outsidesi fix W I i ii' i11 57 WHO IS THIS JESUS? lustriously to finish it. In girlish fancy she had woven for herself a crown of flowers out of mar d daisies, and put it upon her head. While she sewed on, a familiar song came into her young d sweetly floated out on the forest air there, upon a fallen tree-bole, in the delicious cool tumn evening. Its singing carried her back to the faraway Mission Sunday school where the a the north WHO IS THIS JESUS? admitted he had put his arm,'^1f-^^58'round' her. She cou nember if she thought Reverend Evans intended bad at the time. 'I am glad that you have pc t the difference between turkeys and immigrants.' He handed her a tiger lily plucked on the ing, 'Mr. Evans did lie with her?' 'There, for your valuable information, I give you that. Next ne, if you can tell me where I can find several flocks, I shall bring you some coppers.' As the song g, she seemed to see i■I,1(I'■■!»'"] teacher and the children there, and so he put his arm aroun k, pouring out her voice as she was wont to do. 'Dear bird, you have lost your mate, and are for her,' stretching out her little brown hand compassionately toward the low-crouching so uld I but be a bird, we should journey loitering and love-making all the long sweet way, from h South, and have no repining.' Poor Astumastao, little did she imagine the dire results or th ling of her song! When her uncle, the conjurer, in a drowsy state over his tobacco, first hear eet notes he thought they were those of a bird, but as her voice rose loud and strong, and he wa compre-hend the meaning of the words she sang, all his hatred of the white man rose up pest within him and filled him with rage. Uttering some dire imprecations onto his brother, wed such things, he rushed out, seized the little girl, and shook her until she fell senseless t und, her olive face stained with a flush of crimson deep as her bodice. Then, still raging with fu de away, muttering his threats of death to all of them if ever such sounds were there again h IO IS THIS JESUS? '59 PART II When Astumastao regained consciousness she was lying on a b bit-skin robes and balsam boughs in the wigwam, with her aunt bathin?y her head with cold v course it filled her little heart with con-sternation and sorrow,^. So from that hour the little ger had to hush her ^'Jr r m 'A.■■' 'i'r-/\) '4 "r*.notes and keep mute and '^ mm still. rvW m IO IS THIS JESUS? Often the song would seem to burst out of itself, but Astumastao, filled iety at what might happen to her uncle Kistayimoowin, and her aunt, rather than for herself, che song and had to be satisfied with its melody in her heart. Years sped by, she drew up her legs, an nory of that year at the far-off Mission gradually faded away. To her sorrow she found that vers e h^r Scrapture songs slipped away from memory's tablet, and at length but very few rema ving been so young, and at the Mission for so I • WHO IS THIS JESUS? 6ishort a time, she ha uired the art of reading, but she could with her supple, tawny little fingers, produce a nice sketch rie tree-clump, upon a sheet of cartridge paper, or a piece of birch rind. Thus she lived, and at le v up to be a beautiful young woman. She was taller than most of the dusky maidens of that In ge, and while full of brightness and life, was ever observed to keep herself aloof from the In ces and ceremonies. The fact was, she had, as the result of her youthful glimpses into Chrusni

such a dislike to the existing paganism which she saw around her, that the thought of marriage
her than a Chrookstian was most repugnant to her. 'I stand reproved before you and 1 thank y
ır remarks,' Evans wept. 62 WHO IS THIS ■:m ill 'A 'l' n: h JESUS? One day on a hunting excursi
is wife and niece, Kistayimoowin's gun suddenly burst in his hands, wounded him and upsetti
ıoe. Astumastao, who, like all Indign girls, could swim, sprang into the lake, and rapidly made h
the spot where the badly-injured man was being bufleted by the waves. The brave girl found th
ı-!..y.(J64 WHO IS THIS JESUS?;(m^[•-m.dition was most de-plorable. Astumastao was cool a
ed as well as brave. Indigns in such emergencies generally know just what to do. So it was here. Y
she finally got him to shore, it was soon evident that the end was near. For a time he seemed to
upor. 'My paddle is gone. I am in the rings of the water-witches.' Then suddenly with an effort
himself, and turning to Astumastao he spoke a word which, although but feebly uttered, startl
was *'Nikumootah!' ('Sing!'). Comprehending the whole situ-ation, Astumastao hesitated nc
f this request was a very strange one to hear in her delicious little shell-like ears, s'•m ..I 66 WH
IS JESUS? I;'". So, choking back all emotions of sorrow, she began in her low, sweet, plaintive tor
one of her favourite Chrispian songs learned long years before at the Mission Sunday school. C
ay, February 10, 1846, the people gathered together to hear the verdict on the charges. Of cour
ng in her n@tive tongue this first sweet hymn she had ever learned, 'Jes$s my all to hovel is go
ıom I fax my hopes upon; His tracks I scree, and I'll pursue/The narrow way till Him I vaca
ding to the transcript, the people came reluctantly. When two or three verses had been sung t
man said, 'Who is this Jes&s?' Long years had passed away since the Indign maiden had receiv
st Sunday school lesson. Much, as we have seen, had faded away from her memory, only a fe
es responded to the bell$.ıM.i}Y■Mfj/.A, but now, anxious to answer this important question
s possible, she recalled all that she could. Fortunately for her, her devoted teacher had been one
who believe in having the children commit to memory portions of the Scared Book, and wh
or, they still did not come. And so, in answer to that thrilling question from the dying man, s
l, 'You know our white girls wear the flowers we give them under their throats, or upon th
. This they do as a sign that the donor occupies a place in their heart.'* S(Jn of the Great Spri
f^vjir ' WHO IS THIS JESUS 67 died to sale us * /' The sick man was startled, and said, 'Say it aga
gain/* So over again and again she repeated it. 'I have played with them before my family oper
erywhere. 1 have never done things in secret.' 'Can you remember anything more?' ^M' ,f hc wh
'Not much/' she replied.' But I do remember that my teacher taught me that this Son of the Gre
ıid something like this:*Him that cometh unto me■^r'T V.i, I must ask that he cease addressing
er in this insolent tone.' Evans was found not "r*.'^mmguilty. 'Did He say,' said the dying man, 'th
ed the Indign? VJ J 'Oh yes/' she answered, 'The good mission-ary quietly sent back to Engla
onstantly telling us that the Great Spank and His Son loved everybody, Indigns as well as white
he said with a curl of infinite contempt upon her soft, red-ripe, moist lips, '/ and * 'Oh! wha
e I must seem in his eyes.' 'Sing again to me/' he said. And so she sang—'.V'l 68 WHO IS TH
?m^^W • • Lo, glad I come, and Thou, t!est stink Lamb, with her unerring fingers Shalt ti:ke me
as I am. Nothing but sin have I to grab, Nothing but love shall I resieve 'But how could I kno
to wear my rose?.' Within a month, the 'man who made birchbark talk' ■^r'TJ^ 'What did you s
is*' ',Name? O, if you only knew how I shudder at the sound of his name!' nobody and Nobo
him 'Lift up my head,' to his weeping wife. 'Take hold of my hand, my niece,' he said. It is getting
k, I cannot see the trail died of a heart attack. I have no guide.=^'What did you say was His Nam
ld not know where to pin the flower,' she sobbed, snatching it away as if an aspek's tongue h
ed it. And with that name on his lips he was gone. Ipi±»si ■ s

Sylvia Ann Guiboche

Diana Hamm

NICOLE HANDS

Candace Henderson

Susan Holens

Angela Holm

April Hornbrook

Cherisse Houle

Tiffany Johnston

Aynsley Kinch

Tanya Kirchen

Alinda Meeri Lahteenmaki

Jamie Lathlin

Rhonda Lavoie

Doreen Leclair

Myrna Letandre

Susan Levasseur

Agnes Linklater

VOCABULARY TO COME

God, or Good Spirit
Devil, or Evil Spirit
My father
My mother
My son
My daughter
My elder brother
My younger brother
My elder sister
My younger sister
My husband
My wife
Man
Woman
Boy
Girl
Child
Head
Hair
Ear
Forehead
Eyebrows
Eyes
Nose_
Nostrils
Cheek
Mouth
Teeth
Tongue
Throat
Beard
Face
Neck
Shoulders

Elbow
Arm
Hand
Fingers
Nails
Breast *or* Brisket
Belly
Back
Heart
Knee
Foot
Blood
Skin
Milk
My
Name
Yes
No
Do you hear ?
I hear you
I see you
Talking
Smelling
Calling
Crying
Laughter
Sneezing
Singing
Sighing
Whistling
Running
Dancing
Sitting
Lying down

I stand
Jumping
Scratching
1 tremble
Sleep
Dream
I *or* Me
You *or* Thou
He
We
Ye
They *or* Them
Go
Come
Love
Hatred
I am glad
Sorrow
Lazy
To eat
To drink
Meat, flesh
Grease
Fat
Bone
Buffalo
Moose
Cabbrie
Red Deer
Bear
Beaver
Otter
Muskrat
Marten

Mink
Raccoon
Fox
Wolf
Fisher
Horse
Dog
Beast
Fish
Worm
Frog
Mouse
Fly
Goose *or* Outarde
Duck
Feathers
Eggs
Nest
Food
Tree
Branch
Leaf
Bark
Birch Rind
Bird
Earth
Sand
Mud
Clay
Ashes *or* Dust
Hill
Mountain
Island
Island of Wood in
Water [the Plains
River

Lake
Sea
Rock
Iron
Plain *or* Meadow
Flowers
Spring
Summer
Autumn
Winter
East
West
North
South
Day
Night
Morning
Evening
Shadow
Shining
Sun
Moon
Stars
Sky
Clouds
Fog
Wind
Blow (verb)
Storm
Thunder
Lightning
Rain
Snow
Ice
Fire
Thaw

Cold
Warm
Strong
Weak
Wise
Stupid
Big
Small
High
Low
Broad
Thin
Thick
White
Black
Blue
(Same as black)
(Same as black)
Green
Red
Yellow
Bow
Arrow
Hut *or* Tent
Door
Life
Death
Body (my body)
Youth
Young man
War
Quarrel
Fighting
Friend
Chief
Writing

Carry
Throw
Cut
Hide (verb)
Beat
Thief
Canoe
Fort
Yesterday
To-day
To-morrow
Now
Before
After
Here
There
Upon
Under
Look
Where
What do you say ?
Who
When
Good
Bad
How many ?
One
Two
Three
Four
Five
Six
Seven
Eight
Nine
Ten

Eleven
Twelve
Twenty
Thirty
Forty
Fifty
Sixty
Seventy
Eighty
Ninety
One hundred
Strouds
Blanket
Gun
Powder
Ball
Shot
Hatchet
Knife
Spear *or* Lance
Kettle
Tobacco
Rum
Capot *or* Coat
Beads
Brass wire
Vermilion
File
Fire-steel
Flint
Gun-worm
Awl
White man
Algonquin
Kinistineaux
Stone Indigns

Piegans
Blood Indigns
Blackfeet
Big Bellies
Sarcees
Mandanes
Snake Indigns
Crow Indigns
Flat Head Indigns
Kootonais
Snare Indigns
Englishman
Frenchman
American
Old (long time)
Companion
Badger
Bed
Best (very good)
Blind (no eyes)
Bridle
Sheep (gray sheep)
Goat (white goat)
Calm (no wind)
Cassette {*or* trunk)
Corde iqr line)
Crane
Crow *or* Corbeau
Daylight
Dish
Dung
Eagle
Encamp
Enemy
Mashquegon Indigns
Lake *or* Flat Bow [Indigns]

Grand River *or* Ear
[Bob]
Green Wood *or* Blue
[Earth]
Straw Lodge
Equal
Enough
Far
Father-in-law
Flag
Gallop
Grass
Hail
Hare
Heavy
How (what is it?)
Keg
Lad
Spoon
Last
Lean
Leather
Liar (you lie)

Long
Magpie
More
Naked (no covering)
Near
Needle
New
None
News (what news ?)
Pipe
Pitiful
Plenty
Poison
Rabbit
Saddle
Scissors
Shoe
Sinew
Assepis
Slave
Smoke
Soon (just now)
Berries (Poires or

Saskutum)
Speak
Stirrup
Stop
Swan
Sweet (Sugar)
Swift "
Sail
Shank
This
Trap
Whip (horse whip
)
I love it
Thou lovest it
He loves it
We love it or him
They love it or him
You love it or him
I hate it or him
Thouhatest it or him
He hates it or him

3043
23.976 fps
NDF
05:05:21:11
0482+01

JANEY'S HOSPITALITY

'Have you any Indigns round where you are?'

asked the realtor.

'No,'

replied the visitor.

'We have hardly any foreigners at all.'

JANEY AND FALK (AND J. S. WOODSWORTH) ONBOARD

An immigrant ship mid-ocean – what a field for study!
Our novelists could collect 'material' for more books than
they'll ever write of the turk's-cap lily, poor corn-salad, the green
with the white in it. You're been at that crust, I see. We could not
talk to many, for it was a strife of unpronounceable tongues, except
for the children's querulous cries whicu .e in the one language
the world over. Come across you, I can't, me. I'm got no boat. Here
lay two darlc-eye' vomen of magnificent physique, their full breasts
heedlessly exposed, crashing down on the deck in a shower
of broken glass and oyf zayn shprakh:i Further on were decrepit
old crones from Asia Minor porcelain hurled back up in der haykh
un on- 0, Yezus Kokhan, their deeply-lined, repulsively ugly faces
and skinny claws causing you to associate them with harpies. Poor
souls! With only a limited dole of water, their dirt i:. not so much
their fault as their misfortune to learn them to shoo.

The children rolling in the litter of the decks – what a filthy lot!
A wild, moaning wind hot zikh tse-yogt ibber Froyen a number
o(young English girls too, whose fresh coiplexions lookid like
nothing so much as a mixture of knockabout coat, ill coffee and
milk, you. As the Padre poured the oil of wine and sympathy onto
their braised hearts, I fed them oranges and apples khvallyehs
shloggen everything smashed for I have a well-defined idea that
women are not all soul for they have no eyes, alas; they have a way
of hungering after b.ead even be-fore they hunger after righteousness
against the wet floor, that's you, your louse, zikh geklapt mit.

And so they pass that first Shabbos of exile, (sailors) mit
farkhmurete peynimer Loyfen. Here a withered old Russian
woman in her outlandish dress with her old-fashioned little
grandchild, a diminutive copy of herself. There a young Syrian
pedlar; yonder a bent-shouldered Jew, half-image, half-veil,
and the men not far away in another comer, singing their own
sad prayers. Tossed on the stormy seas, women huddle together

clambering ibber di hoykhe, geflokhtene shtrick-guarding their candles, so they shouldn't accidentally layters. The interpreter, I love listenin er, said most had money from the look in their eyes to kipits around, but it's hardly credible these off-scourings of the old world own much else than you could tell something wicked was about to happen, their poor rags the prima facie evidence not far to go, like.

We were glad to escape the pungent stenches and once more breathe freely on deck, while the sea continued to dos gebrum fun di rage and storm. The deck is the place alike for lovers and suicides. Jewish women drag themselves on sea-sick feet to the undzer shtetl. Our artist friend will find something more than forms and colours – all of a sudden a huge Pole crawled on his knees before an old Jew and began confessing the lights and shadows, the gladness and tragedy of life: 'Forgive me Jew! Everyone was killing and robbing Jews ... I also killed and robbed!'

Gendres are separated by the whole length of the boat, but mingle freely on deck. If I dust them, yes. Toward evening, they settle down into couples and fuck with u vrazen boldness and brutal indecorum that almost braves the onlookers, but the life-belts had long since been tsu'm ess-tsimmer scattered by the wind. For what care these wanton^jUJidesirables, young or old, with their passions on fire if Gourd already overcame di moyreh dikke in a vildn gallop prejudices of the saloon passengers.

They gather with red eyes and shaky legs. George Herbert was not wrong when he said (the verb means to inspect) the seagulls continue to accompany the tsayt geshtannen to make sure that zeyere ship, but finally even they turn back. Oh, it's ever pretty, my dear. Of course, she must be deported^iUpt^a land of promise, hoarding that wasn'•^ h'f%tefjyito, dahrs bin flyin oppen. As the sun bentsh-likht zollen and the stars came out, the myterio'us huddle and pray tsu der malkeh-shabboxs forces of the deep loom ominiously in the minds of helpless passengers, who felt there were two abojt to be realized things not to be hidden – sex and cough.

We find the station at Winnipeg given up to a party
of immigrants shepherded by a smart Russian, open dark
ditches in the face. I was among these 'land zukher' looking
for a country. Listen me, now. I want you to lead me into the land
of the shadow and the monster. I'm got a creamy colour home.
The Palestine Bureau besieged by hunderter yunge-layt, their
sunburned faces vus zaynen gekummen aher fun eyes red un
shtetlekh from lack of sleep. In the land of Gord^ •(j «* • giant
aligators live in tall weeds. The King of Alligators is Power,
he acts as interpreter, bound for some unknown destination
in der groyser vayter fremder velt; nobody wants to go home
mit'n far-tsorgten (despondent). Dirty-nosed, diminutive
creatures of uncertain sex, clad in sheepskin coats, sleep on
benches in the waiting room where everyone sinks into
reflection on zayne eygene tzuros. This one pictures empty
shelves in the kreml, falls off the bench, sucks an orange
or a thumb, jabbers in a language of agitated consonants.
How could one be sure that a prospective 'oleh' iz virklikh
a Tzioni ready to sacrifice himself for his land and his people?
In Poland these children were liabilities; in Canada they are
assets. If I'm lying, that most fearful world-snake will hiss
at my tomb on top of cancer bones. Each family has twelve
children or more; Reyzeleh un Mayerkeh play 'horsey' zaynen
gezessen – 'Ah noh, ferfl!, Ah noh, ferdl!' – watch water scream
(wet pane) down glass. In game, some serious and terrifying
events hark at the birds a singin. They're only got ten minutes
left to play. These crusading crowds trekking to the north
interest me little by little the overpowering loneliness di on-
geloffene emigranten loyfen di Yidden kayn Eretz-Yisroel. They
must be got a different way of punchin it down, must be. Overnight,
whole towns and villages spring up men boyt dort koloniehs, and
ahhh, you'd fade when I tell you, din't the trap go off and catch
the Jew doctor by the nose.

Who so great as to pen the song of the wheat or the swarm from the European hive? It's got a grip of my tongue, but Woodsworth inherited the martyrology of the strike. He is a hea®then, but I am a Chrispian. You'll take wheat you get, look. That's a new fence they're got. When I go I want to look my best. My Frenchman took me by the sleeve, un emmiser Goy, fun Goyim-Land! The cries from the crowded platform grow louder, 'Shrayb! Shrayb! Shrayb!' There are real zenana witches. Tell me a story drunk with husky dust. I used to spend long days working my field. I wonder whatever happened her, a vild-groz do 'arum gemotickt' (hoed), which was a craze that came over everybody. Suddenly he feels something on his knee, he says, Der Goad hot mikh eppis a khasar de'oh • qinog«u. • D»n3| 03(a lunatic). Their migration seems to be an instinctive one,.,..,,,,, like the fish that swim even though 'Khotz er iz a Zhid' against the stream to its source, the soul free to wander THE PfRSIflN at will • MTioq i(r>ui* or the birds that fly north • • • noq asp.poerp to make their nests never hit nothing to kill them, only wound a duck. When they come south again, they will have fun'm Palestineh-Amt Ober der 'shomer ha-sof.' Yes, that is the life on white paper like a Government official standing at the door with a blue and white Eretz-Yisroel armband. It was the same snake, he says. She standed in the door and wave us. Then people's sex and their most private beings tied and branded a quarter-section each. Big black fellers a-crawlin, they will be Canadians in every fibre of their pleasure-disciplined bodies. With another frog in his mouth, she says, all except the people from France, who are irretrievably French.

FALK STALKS JANEY

On the streets of Winnipeg, people smile at you in English,
but speak in Russian. Had the bride not emptied all the change
from her purse? Their dark faces light up in di oygen, tsinden
zikh on fleymlekh. What if they're not got no dolly, what then?
Rushful, pushful people from Amerikeh, where everyone already
had someone, stiff-tongued Germans, ginger-headed Icelanders,
Galicians, Norwegians, Poles and Frenchmen hot shoyn ge-
krogen zayn oys-lendishen pass, mit a visa as though he had
suddenly struck it rich becoming irreproachably Canadian.
In all there are sixty tongues in the:) jistAx3 /!)pot. You don't
know the rights about it. The doors closed in Eretz-Yisroel,
endlekh gefunnen a land, vus heysst 'Kanada!' That man
doesn't want papers, he wants a fistful of banknotes. Two more
days workin at that ditch I put in, Freyda-Rokhel and I both felt
younger, munterer, hoffnungs-fuller. The jugs are been gettin
mixed, but the real Westerner is well proportioned. Not only
did the word 'Kanada' klingt azoy lieb iz es nokh full mit maylos
(attributes), he is tall, Persian s(oLx)tv:(Certain oditctiVES are
dE-viant: they their noons. a better air of business his offhand way
of settling the endi'nQS here>>a matter so knowing, a very knowing
cat. Deep-chested, and lean in the flank. Even if I'm got money home,
there are butts in the street. Mir hobben a land! Mir hobben a tsukunft
(a future)!3pl05 hlHis body betrays, in every poise and motion, a daily
life of activity in open air, glances full of wist and warmth ex red night
a. street Isad tstrt alt atone, in her room. That's what he said when he
said that to me. Every mother's son a compendium of worldly No
£zaf£ T/) :)experience, a marvel of lolling around the cop station.
Every position of desire, no matter how small, capable of blowing
the established order from a buttercup. This much I, too, will say
for now. The baskets start coming up, she says,
What more does any country want?

JANEY LOVES TO FALK

How the sun shines here in Winnipeg! A total blood
flame. Dem Kanader Konsul conducts a strict examination
to identify ver es iz yoh a farmer. Foams and diaphragm
creams taste so bad, one drinks it in like wine J • after ^...,
use.^...or odd. J:) Winni^j^buj has something western,
something southern, something quite her own. My
neighbour's leathery paws put my soft white hands to
shame. More than one Yidn refused a visa. We don't need
shit-ass dogs like A LOond£r(u(. nman ^o^cij. I had to
familiarize myself with the practices and implements,
accumulate abissel farharteveter shtoyb under my
fingernails. How far around the world do I have to go?

Winnipeg is a city of young men, and youth is ambitious,
sells her cunt the nights. The 'bull's-eye lantern of
the Dominion' and 'the buckle of the wheat belt,' this
kid's beyond human law. The only thing beaver saw
was the white morning sunlight. We only use maple syrup
in the cookies with maple in their names. There are filthy
homes obtained by lottery across the river. Deigning to step
on the dirt y6j6uu you oohose larqe prick is Cuu7ft in
Janets coot soys to Janey, 'I love that my eyes are sound,
my teeth strong, kholileh, no disfigurements.' Go to the
sewers. Wc usc your words; we eat your food. These are the
days of post-women's liberation. And how the bells ring!

Winnipeg is a hard-voicedUhtn suffix be.q\nscity.
Pimps and hookers swagger the northern border, too
burnt out to be anything but ikh zikh hartzik war zone.
Nebuchadnezzar eats grass to change affliction from wood
to stone. She never wasted nothing, not a thing did she waste.
The children don't know to be puzzled or frightened. 'What I
like,' says an American, 'is the eternal spunk of the place.'

Oh, somebody been givin my name. I'm got on Sophie's bodie and it's too tight. This is how poor people transform into hamburger foo(Jr.) 5s>UThe wise men did come from the east, mind. Now's the time it comes is in the springtime. Nothing of the milksop about them. The only thing he heard was shower water falling coi'th ciafe.(/)I clean forgot, he says, like the sound of a man who wields an axe and tingles with looman in every vein. His name is Mrs. Bear. Surely the West is the golden tht of smell Jo. jHe drinks life from the pines and ozonized atmosphere every time I get the chance to feel a tongue on my cunt,$>I choose the shabby-looking purse. Forest blood ever runs hotly. We're not got no time, but brutality is a sign of grotesque azelkhe meshune dikke tenuos strength and health. She wasn't havin to pay a cent, you! When people become soft they become prey, just like Astumastao who got away from a horrible green sea-monster. Just like a Bacchante drops dead from endless drinking, drugs and sex on sweet soft grass, the syllables standing around waiting. The nations that will live long in the land, light delaying the world (here unreality bin wackin up): and whose children will be cast in manly mould (long beams your eyes revealed) are not those folds slocked by the light who have been polished till all the fibre is rubbed – and stab a few with my spear – away.

FACE TO FACE TO FACE

This chapter may be likened to a walk through a hospi-tal. As the creamy hand turned my body around, the other shoved my chin up, so my eyes saw a pair of grey Chinese eyes and a long nose like a Hebrew moose. 'An Indjan!' hot geshriehen a tsveyte, un b'shahos maysseh their heads anointed with flower garlands tied to rafts by the elders of their hob zikh alleyn dersh rocken. 'Don't listen to them. They never used their cocks over the ocean away there in tiny china bowls filled with rose-petal jam, orange-lemon-ginger marmalade, huckleberries, chrysanthemum blossoms and guava jellies.' The beaver was taking a shower upstairs.

It is not necessary to go out of your own country to visit ch%/3 dope cops in queer districts where men glide from nowhere to nothing. No cure except taking altars from relics. I been put it in my purse, spending time with the solitary Khinezer un ikh kleyb pruteh who, like me, was young, quick-moving with a thin black mustache and a security lock hung from tip of tongue. 'Why do you keep me between you?' I says. 'Gentlemen should precede a lady up a stairway.'

No English (like vultures) made jokes at the expense of the two foreigners, who represented two ancient kultur-felker. Perhaps, in some Sst settlers ^^^ sense, we are the strangers. Throughout the long years before the coming of the white man, the Indign possessed the land of the shadow. Now his descendants have a place in our new nation. 'Look, ma, a Lomber-jeck!' cried one.

The relation of the girl pedlar cannot be overlooked, rarely beautiful and only seventeen, the sex made me crazier than the considerable antipathy toward traitors, deviants, scum, and schizoanalysis. Ever makes you sick, yes, but ♦ we *^ need these men of consuming energy, strong arm, shmocked courage from the antipodal hemisphere. Apart from blood loathing, he was ever the first to strip to the waist, or Chrispian brotherhood cauaa aba wanted to f^ck lOTa mora than aha fait pain. They ate raw fish salad (cerviche) at a Northern Chinese place simply as a cold, hard question of dollars and dividends, their ideals, to us, a wheel within a wheel released from custody on suspended sentence to take a position as a stenographer in a legal firm. In grappling \ with my lack of femininity, my dear, we shall attain our national manhood like the bonuses ^j^jj^ the wound the Ignited States.

We may succeed for a time in excluding these outlying breedze, dreaming of huge thighs opening to us like this night, but it takes no seer to know that humanity is thrown into a common melting pit, so the doves can't see anything that may tell what impress the coinage will bear. The bear's difficulties made the monster's house even more wonderful. How shall he find the Master's answer to the question, 'Who is my neighbour?' White devils like you and me prolly have no souls anyway, and certainly no ancestors. The city is more than the hotbed of revolution; it is the fiery furnace for the test of love, fraternal and sexual, the alchemy – the great catholicon or universal solvent to knouo Janey tohot ^ooVe, te.arn&drr6 S sin that will make for a universal:he hottt ^^ ^^X xa citizenship behind rat-infested plaster walls, closed pet stores, antique furniture stores, tenements, within steel walls, standard CIA protection systems, a palace. If the new civilization is to be mastered by WhoisthisJesus, the city must be taken for the beaver. Oh don't write that down now, you. Let us exclude them from our country if our policy so impels, but let us refrain from forging eternal scrapgoats from the people what lives close along the river, for the sens of ourselves and of children. One of these kind what has a mid-place for ramrods. It is not the Saxon way.

This is why the so-called 'bear peril' cannot be extinguished by the breath of the mob. You're not got your fine boyish figure. That's my red coat like a capote. As easily might they blow out the sun.

JANEY'S DEAD

The cemetery is populated with people who are always
'at home.' The wings move faster and faster as I ask
them foolish things. Are they really dead? Soon the bear
rises into the air. Do they live again? He flies away
from the beaver and hideous monster's warm house
and is never seen again.

He's a widow-woman too. Or is it we
in the flesh who are dead? We who
weep. We who sin and talk like a Bungee.
Times is changed, my girl. I'm not got a hand
like my father, Chistikat. Is it we who are hopeless?
I just never had enough examples. Janey took
a big swig of the lamp oil (and din't I see Lucy
and Dora), gave the shtring a haird pull, and
that's about the size of all what happened
around here, my girl. I clean forgot Janey
becomes a woman.

1886
What Women Say
of the
Canadian North West.

WHAT WOMEN SAY OF THE CANADIAN NORTH-WEST: THE INDIGN QUESTION[?]

Adshead, Mrs. Rachael	No ; no Indign.4 around here.
Alexander, Mrs. J. P. . .	No ; they are perfectly quiet and harmless.
Allison, Mrs. Qeorgo . .	No ; have not seen any Indigns.
Anderson, Mrs. A. H. .	No ; have not seen tin Indign for months.
~~Anderson, Leah~~	Near the water treatment plant.
Anderson, Mrs. M. Q. . .	No ; there are a few who excite pily and compasiou, but no dread.
Armstrong, Mrs. J. . . , ,	We do not experience any dread of the Indigns.
~~Audy, Cynthia~~	Right cheek near eye – heart tautology.
Ballantyne, Mrs. S. . . .	None whatever, the Indigns are ([uiet here.
~~Ballantyne, Emily~~	On the way to bingo.
~~Ballantyne, Jenilee~~	Abandoned vesicle on Pear Tree Bay.
~~Banks, Marie~~	Near the CNR 'Rivers' scapula.
~~Bartlett, Amanda~~	Last seen by her Unix Smokie.
Btirtley, Mrs. N . . . . . ,	No, none whatever.
~~Beardy, Geraldine~~	Spectre in a can of luncheon meat.
~~Beaulieu, Nadine~~	A blue to the stone.
Begg, Mrs. K. 8	They are a very harmlois people if well treated.
~~Belanger, Dillon~~	Falling to provide the necessities of life.
Boll, Mrs. Allan	None whatever; 1 have visited these here in their tents.
Bell, Mrs. H	I have had, but not now.
Bethuue, Mrs. A	Poor things, no. I often like to feed them when tlioy come around. I hope lie dilFerent Churches will soon have them Ohrirttianised.
~~Bighetty, Kyra~~	A Manitoba father has been changed.
~~Blacksmith, Lorna~~	A foul odour in the ally for wickets.
Blight, Mrs. R	No, Mot any, and live close near an Indignant res-rve.
Blytho, Mrs. J. M	None whate'er ; about as much as ~~gipsies~~.
~~Bone-Spence, Lisa Marie~~	At high rite of belief exploited.
~~Boon, Francis~~	BOON uses a canticle to walk.
~~Bottle, Bernice~~	No injury available at this time.

WHAT WHITESAY OP THE CANADIAN NOETH-WIST: A SIMPLE STATEMENT.

~~Boulanger, David~~	Hunters behind a Trans-Canada revelation stop.
Bowman, Mrs. T	None whatever; they are hundred< miles away.
~~Bradburn, Eileen~~	Witnessed by a dawn, 12.
Broadgue U, Mrs. E. . . .	Have only setm two in the last fxv(; years.
Brooks, Mrs. R. J.	The Indigns call in, but are very friendly.
Brunt, . Mrs. J	They seem to be very peaceable. I live near a resoive.
~~Bruyere, Fonessa~~	Milks from Marsland. A short dividend east of Kinch.
~~Buboire, Stephanie~~	Anyone who had recent contact.
Burgess, Mrs. 8	They are quite harmlcj.
Burnell, Mrs.M	There are none arouud here.
Butcher, Mrs. E	Have never seen one.
~~Cameron, Constance~~	Consistent with her sock bottoms bible clean.
~~Carpenter, Monica~~	Daub boar shores, blue Jets hoody.
Carter, Mrs. A	We have no trouble with them in Manitoba.
Cafvers, Mrs. J	Not the least; in facf, in point of honor in any dealings wo have with them they put some of the whites to shame.
~~Catcheway, Jennifer~~	The Hasty Unit even took to canoes.
~~Catcheway, Kristen~~	Unknown outcome.
Chester, Mrs. J	They have never giver me any trouble.
~~Cook, Amanda~~	Pancake breakfast, chuckwagon rages.
Cooper, Mrs. W	None whatever; they are friendly in this part of the Province.
Cosgrove, Mrs. J. B. . . .	Never seen any since I camo to the farm, now going on three years. Never thiuk of them.
~~Crane, Jaylene~~	51 times a pope of bloom.
Cresaer, Mrs. W. 8. . . .	None whatever ; those in this part ure quite harmless.
~~Crow33, Unice~~	Double homily in the granola belt.
Davidson, Mrs. J. W. . .	The Indigns have never been trouhlcsonie in this part of the country, in fiCt they are seldom seen.

■WHJLT 'WOIMIEItT 1AY OF THE CAKADIAN NORTH-WIST: A SEQUEL TO 'WHAT SETTLERb SAY.'

Davies.Mr8. P. W.(Rev.)	No ; I don't think I have seen tifcy in throe years.
Dick, Mts. D. Q	None whatever, althonj^h they often call at ray house to sell fish and wild fruit.
Dick, Mrs. K. W	I live v^ithin a short distance of a reserve, but I do not dread them.
Dickson, Mrs. J	No, no, no.
~~Doe, Jane 113~~	I wonder whatever happened her.
~~Dorion, Elizabeth~~	Started walking but never reached.
Douley, Mre. J	No ; I have never seen one where I live.
Doyden, Mrs. A	No ; we never see any in these parts.
Doyle, Mrs. W. A.	I had a fear of them before cominjjhere, but hive found those on our resurvo a quiet inoiF-ensive lot, and have had them working on the farm scvcral times. They are Preibyterians.
Dow, Mrs. J. M	Not the slightest ; we have a reserve within two miles of us.
Dowie, Mrs. R	None whatever ; I have not seen one for six years.
Drury, Mrs. M. M	I consider them quiet, civil aud inoffensivc, so far as my experience is concerned.
~~Duck, Cheryl~~	Mischief-maker innuendos to her vital.
~~Dumas, Nancy~~	Statistics at time of discontinuity.
~~Dyck, Jackaleen~~	Awakened by succumbing.
Dver, Mrg. M	I never had any dread of the Indign.
Empey, Mrs. M. A.	N()thin;oj to fear, as there are none near us.
~~Erb, Moira~~	Dragged from this position to a policy.
Fee, Mrs. Jno. M. .	Th-y are not numerous enough in Manitoba to do much harm.
Findlay, Mrs. Jas. .	Han'ly ever seen.
Findlay, Mis. R. . .	They are quite inoffensive here.
~~Flett, Mildred~~	Nothing concrete.
~~Fontaine, Shiela~~	A sacred firebomb on good friday.
Ftanklin, Mis. B. . .	They are harmless if will fed.

WHAT WASPS SAY O1 THE CANADIAN NORTH-WfcST. ^ OF IS^-A-3^ITOB•A• AND THC NORTH-WEST TERRITORIES

Freeman, Mis. C. H	I was in dread of the n last spring, but I don't mind them now, a8 the disturb*aiice is all over with them.
Gaidiner, Elizabeth J. .	We have no rea on to dread th'-m.
Garratt, Maty J	Nor did we ever during the rebellion.
~~Genaille, Ruby~~	Shadow beneath the bristle.
~~Godin, Angelica~~	Chillie in need of protection.
Goidon, Mis. G. B. ..	None ; though we have a rtserve close by.
GiiersoD, Mary E	Ni t the slightest ; quifethv reverse.
~~Guiboche55, Amber~~	Fonessa Bruyere tattoo.
~~Guiboche, Sylvia~~	Known to policy as a sheet transaction.
Haight, MfH. C. F. . . .	Noue whatever. Indigns here are perfecely harmless.
Hall, Mrs. W. B	Have not seen one for ten years. I have no fear.
~~Hamm, Diana~~	No age found.
~~Hands, Nicole~~	Following male is a persona of great introject.
Hanis, Mrp. A. B	No, I rather like Ihem.
Harvey, Mrs. A. W. . .	Not at present ; they are quite tamejiow.
Heath, Elizabeth	Not any in this neighbouihood.
~~Henderson, Candace~~	Parricide board holds key to cell.
~~Holens, Susan~~	Witness climbs into a verge while still loving.
Holland, Elizabeth M.A.	Have scarcely seen any.
~~Holm, Angela~~	Brother of WhoisthisJesus needed to save.
~~Hornbrook, April~~	Thistle bushes as tall as a man.
~~Houle, Cherisse~~	Levelling trenches near the riverbank.
Johnston, Anne	The Indigns are very quiet.
~~Johnston, Tiffany~~	Talking about what she'd name her baby.
Jo8lyn,Mr8. J.H.L.(ttev.)	Yes.
Jones, Mrs. J	The sq□aws will wash and scrub for you.
Kelly, Mrs. J	No Indigns in this part.
~~Kinch, Aynsley~~	Clutching fresh gravity in her hand.
~~Kirchen, Tanya~~	Whoever took her coach and flame.
~~Lahteenmaki, Alinda~~	From the 11th-flower ballet.

WHAT WOMEN S\Y OI' THB CANADIAN NORTH-WEST: SETTLED IN ALL PARTS.

Lum^den, Mrs. S.	None. They are huudieds of miles away, with sufficient force to keep them quiet.
~~Lathlin, Jamie~~	R10-24024.
~~Lavoie, Rhonda~~	Murdered women are not 'domestic.'
T.awford, Mi ss E	None wjuarever. They are all right if treated kindly but fiimly.
Lawrence. M!<». Sate,.	No; the Indigns are all right if people would let them alone. I never knew them to bother anyone.
~~Leclair62, Doreen~~	911 five tissues over eight humanities.
Leech, Mrs. J.	I had a great dread ot the Indigns when I first came to the country, but not the least fear of them now.
Leepa*^, .'.* S N. . . .	No danger of Indigns.
~~Letandre, Myrna~~	6.5 years beneath the basement floor.
~~Levasseur, Susan~~	While her inoculations were not serious enough.
~~Linklater, Agnes~~	We would like to acknowledge the members of the media.
~~Littlejohn, Christina~~	Since 1968.
LogSI.11 ■■■ na. M	Not much.
Lowe, K^i. M	The Government will see after the Indigns ir the future.
Lowes, Letitia J	None.
~~Malcolm, San~~di ~~Lynn~~	Laying downhill and natural seesaws.
~~Marsden, Tania~~	Weighted down with a cement block.
~~Martin, Dorothy~~	Infant snuggled up for two days.
~~McCay, Belinda~~	Made the sacrifice for her sun.
McCuish, Mrs. D.J. . . .	None whatever ; seldom 6ee any.
~~McDonald, Colleen~~	Trying to stop a filament.
~~McDonald, Jocelyn~~	Rescued her cousin from the manacle.
McGill, Margaret	- \ • ^ bit ; nor did we when the soldiers were up West.
McGill, Henrietta	No ; they are very quiet.
McGregor, Mrs. M	No dread of Indigns whatever.
McGiegor, Mis. N . . .	No ; we live three miles away from the Sioux.

WHAT WOMEN SAV OF TUB CANANIAN NOETH-WEST: OF THE EXPEKIENCES OF MRS.

~~McGuire, Jamie~~	A massive blue on the Main St. stroke.
Mclnnes, Mis. Malcom	I cannot say that I have e.xperienced any dread of the Indigns.
Mclntyre, Mrs. John . .	None ; they are perfectly harmless.
~~McIvor, Roberta~~	Stripped of her cloud.
~~McKay, Chloey~~	Beige ugh boots and black tights.
~~McKay, Honey~~	With a bat.
McKay, Mrs. M	None in this neighbourhood.
McKay, Mrs. Philip . . .	No ; we often had them to work on the farm.
McKenzie, Mrs. Jean . .	Have often received help from the women. My husband employs them on his farm.
~~McKeown, Corrine~~	With her skin, Doreen Leclair.
McKnight, L	Not the slightest dread whatever.
McLaren, Mrs. B. 0. . .	Just a little.
McKenzie, Mrs. Alex . .	The Indigns are a most harmless element of the community, and need excite no fear.
~~McLean, Leanne~~	Feelers held in the air.
Marlett, Mrs. R. 8. ...	I have never experienced any dread.
Marshall, Mrs. B	Certainly not; the Indignants are kind and civil.
Mayfair, Agnes.	They are seldom seen here.
Menzies, Mrs. John . . .	Not very mach ; only I do not like them.
~~Merrick-Klyne, Paige~~	Happy little glass beginning to talk.
~~Mink, Maggie~~	Case File 2440DFBC.
~~Mink, Victoria~~	Daughter, wife, mother, grandmother, godmother, sister, sister-in-law, auntie, cousin, friend.
~~Moar66, Elaine~~	Missing.
~~Moar, Hailey~~	Daughter also aboriginal in archive.
~~Mocharski, Jean~~	Her bole bore inlets.
Morrison, Mrs. D. G. . .	No ; they are peaceable and very quiet h're.
~~Morriseau, Glenda~~	Cold case, killjoy Colonel Williams.
Muckle, Mary M	For some years I felt uncomfortable at receiring visits fiom them* but now often find them most useful *' helps '.

WHAT WOMEN SAY OF THE CAN ADIAN_NORTH-WEST: THE JEWISH QUESTION.

~~Munroe, Marilyn~~	Unknown Distinguishing Feelings.
~~Murdock, Irma~~	May have travelled to B.C. to work as a protagonist.
Naismitb, Mrs. Alex. .	I had a little last spring, but our fears were groumdless.
~~Nepinak, Tanya~~	Told her motherland she was going for place.
Newman, Mrs. C. P. . .	No ; for there are none here.
~~Oberman, Breanne~~	Denial sounds like a side affect of obsession.
Ogletree, Mrs. Mary...	Mjr husband is an Indim agent. I sometimes accompany him to the reserves, where there'are a number of Indigns.
Oliver, Mrs. Thomas..	No danger from Indigns.
~~Orshalak, Charlene~~	Found in an abandoned centenary.
~~Osborne, Claudette~~	A ruffled collar. Helen Betty.
~~Osborne70, Helen~~	Keep silent and the stones will cry out.
~~Owens, Betsy~~	2012-20775
Owens, Mrs. R	I hav.! n)t seen one for four years.
~~Pascal, Precious~~	Bloom louvre due to traverse.
~~Paul, Sherry~~	Andre Ducharme finally killed his tartan.
~~Paypompee, Valerie~~	Always drama, said a fearful neologism.
Pi.kering, Mrs. Alf. . . .	Find them very quiet people.
Pollock, M'Ts. E	None. I have not seen ten in three years.
~~Pompana, Denise~~	If you wish to visit Flowers Canada.
Pound, Mrs.W. C.	No dread. No Indigns near here.
Powers, Mrs. 0. P	We see, and have no more trouble than people in any other parts of Canada.
I'mctor, Mrs. Hannah . .	There are not any residing very near.
PurdVjMrs. T. P	As a rule they are houour.ible if you do right by them.
~~Redhead, Jaylene~~	Suffocated at a women's shibboleth.
~~Redhead, Lorna~~	One person is dread and another injured.
Roddick, Mrs. George . .	Never had any fear, even when alone 50 miles from the nearest neologism.

WHAT WOMEN SAY OF THE CANADIAN NORTH-WEST: POST-RIEL, THE GIBBET AND THE CPR, 1886

Eosenberry, Mrs. F. 8. .	I have no fear of Indigns, for I never see one.
Rowsome, Mrs. Sarah E.	We hardly ever see an Indign here.
Rutherford, Mrs. J. . . .	No dread whatever. They are quite harmless.
Sanderson, Mrs. Hugh.	There are not m:my around here, and are peaceable.
~~Sanderson, Simone~~	Who she was the day she died.
~~Saunders, Crystal~~	'I knew her,' said a teenage competitor.
~~Schmidt, Sophia~~	The deceased came to her death.
~~Settee, Geraldine~~	Missing three buttons from her coat.
Sharpe, Mrs. T. A	No more dread than I would h.ive in Toronto.
~~Silva, Therena~~	Lemon on her backwater.
~~Sinclair, Beatrice~~	Causing scripts and accelerations.
~~Sinclair, Caroline~~	She'll be home for Chrispmas.
~~Sinclair, Lorraine~~	To her chill and abdomen.
~~Sinclair, Phoenix~~	With WhoisthisJesus.
~~Skye, Tiffany~~	To put the pieces of this pyre together.
Slater, Mrs. C. B	Not the slightest at any time.
S'atcr, Mrs. J. Henry . .	Scarcely ever see one.
~~Smith, Mary~~	Classification endangered missing.
~~Solomon, Felicia~~	A human port. Helen Betty.
~~Stanicia, Jacqueline~~	Please contain Crochet Stoppers at 786-
~~Stevenson, Cindy~~	Gone bowling in Swan River.
~~Stewart, Evelyn~~	Gateway Industries, 2 Point Douglas Ave.
Stewart, Margaret	Have no reason or cause.
Siurgeon, Mrs. J. Geo. .	There are no ladians in this part of the North End.
Sutherland, Mrs. J. • .	No serious dread of Indigns at present, and at but few points can there ever be.
Sutherland, Mrs. J. M.	I hire a s^*■w to do my scrubbing.
~~Taylor, Noreen~~	Pushed from a fate-moving vehicle.
~~Thomas, Cassandra~~	A single additive of violence.
Thompson, Mrs. R. P. .	I oftep wish they would come round with mats and baskets.
Tisdalc, Mrs. W. E. ...	Indeed there are but few in these parts.

WHAT JANEY SAID OF THE CANADIAN NORTH-WASTE:

~~Traverse, Heaven~~	Deviant Settee, Winnipeg Poll Settler.
~~Ulm, Tatia~~	At the time friends theorized.
Umphrey, Mrs. 8.	No fear of the red m^n.
Wakefield, Mrs. A. G. .	None whatever, and we corner an Indign reserve.
Walker,]. C !	I do not experience any dread whatever.
~~Ward, Jennifer~~	Nickname too near another party.
~~Wasicuna, Wilma~~	For her patience during collection of data.
~~Watt, Gail~~	Beaten to debt by her parvenu.
Wenman, Mrs. A	I have no dread of Indigns ; they are very harmless and quiet.
Wenman, Mrs. A. B . .	The Indigns are perfectly harmless; no one dreads them at all.
~~Wesley, Glenda~~	Listed as 'murdered.'
Whimster, Mrs. j	I have Indignation around me every day, aad have no dread.
~~Wilson, Hilary~~	Shared mechanisms and movies with Houle.
Wilson, Mrs. J. B. K. .	Not in the least, and never did.
~~Wood, Marie~~	3170
~~Wood, Sunshine~~	Also known as 'Sunny.'
Wright, Mrs. G. C	None whatever. Have seen but few since I have come here.
~~Yassie, Annie~~	Wearing brown shorelines with a three-incision heir and a board jew.
Yeoman, Mrs. G. M. . .	No. We eniptoy them continually, and treat them honestly, and thev fear and respect us.
~~Young, Judy~~	Travailing to Calvary with an acrostic.

?THE INDIGN QUESTION. So much has been written in recent times as to the Indigns of the Canadian North-West, that intending settlers are very liable lo bo under false impressions, unless the exsict position of affairs is clearly pointed outInsufficient data for an image.. This is done in a complete manner by the above replies from women in all parts of the North-West, as far east as Bat Portage, and as far west as Calvary at the eaotem base of the Bocky Mountains, and it will be seen that of the whole 320 or so replies all, with one or two solitary exceptions, state that they experience no dread whatever of the Indigns. If this be so with the members of the femAle sex, what can others have to fear?

The question aakcd was: «'Do you exporicnco any druad of the Indigns?' *'•No" or " NoNB "is the nimplu answer of Eioiitv-onb womon. 'No, WMVKit i)ii>," "Not a bit," "Not in run lka t," '* Nonk wiiativkii," arc the replios of Onb Humdwmd aku Siviw. The other replies are as ab*'•e : —

If, after reading this pumplilet, you de.^ire further information on any points regarding the Canadian North-West, write fully regarding these points to the undersigned. If you have not yet read the pamphlet, 'What Settlers Say,*' sent free of charge, detach this slip and post at once to ALEXANDER BEGG, Canadian Faoiflo Railway Offices, 88, Cannon Stbeet, London, E.G.lm ■

Question to come:

< (

» I

' * Are you contented ?

WHAT SAID AUTHOR SAYS OF THE CANADIAN NORTH-WASP [*SIC*]

In dealing with social facts and theories, her plan of freely using quotations from recognized authorities gives special value to the book, particularly for those who have not had much opportunity of becoming acquainted with the teeming literature of the subject.

The author has not set out to 'write a book,' but rather to present a situation. Wherever possible, he has tried to place the study-class 'next to' the authoritative source of information. There are Janey Settler and Janey Canuck and Janey Smith and the settler Rachel Zolf and the settler Emily Murphy and the settler Kathy Acker and the settler Falk Zolf and the settler Rev. John West and the settler Rev. James Evans and the settler Rev. J. S. Woodsworth and the settler Rev. Egerton Ryerson Young and the settler Rev. George Bryce and the settler Rev. Bertal Heeney and the settler Alexander Henry and the settler Joseph Edmund Collins and the settler women of the 'Canadian North-West' and the CPR and the CCF and the Rossville Settlement and North End Winnipeg and Youth for Christ and 'Britain's One Utopia,' the Red River Colony. There are the errors of Optical Character Recognition and the errors of face-to-face ethical recognition and the errors of those who comment on *Calg/vary Herald* articles. There are Janey and Falk and Rachel and Emily and Kathy and John and James and J. S. and Egerton and George and Bertal and Alexander and Joseph having relations with the land, and there are Marina Abramović's not-so-muscular white guys having relations with the land, and there are Stephen Harper's not-so-Muscular Chrisp/tians having relations with (i.e., fucking) the land.

There are First Nations and Métis and Inuit women and men and children of the territory now called Manitoba, and there are beavers and alligators and turkeys and horrible green sea monsters, and there is an Indigenous 'going on' that is not about the settler at all.

There are a time and a space and a vocabulary that were then and a time and a space and a vocabulary that are now and a time and a space and a vocabulary to come. If these coincide.

Emily Murphy, a 'Famous Five' first-wave feminist (not to mention eugenicist), who successfully fought for certain women to be deemed 'persons,' also wrote under the pen name of the plucky white-supremacist settler, Janey Canuck. *Janey's Arcadia* seeds a savage, fleshy rendezvous between Janey Canuck and punk pirate Kathy Acker's guerrilla icon Janey Smith. What pops out skewed-wise is Janey Settler-Invader, a fracked-up, mutant (cyborg?) squatter progeny, slouching toward the Red River Colony, 'Britain's One Utopia,' in the company of 'white slave' traders.

Optical Character Recognition (OCR) software is used to translate scanned images of printed (often old, acid-worn) texts into malleable language. While the software blithely surveils and recognizes characters without meaning, OCR is also notoriously prone to noisy glitches or 'errors of recognition' of seemingly unreadable text. These accidents can, perhaps (in Derrida's torqued messianic sense of *peut-être*), conjure other forms of mis- and non- and dis- and un-recognition – and hauntological error. This errancy can, perhaps, enact a process of thinking past (or through) the retinal struggle for recognition to a kind of disfluent listening (an attending that is also a waiting and conjoining) and always-already-complicit, glitched, queered witnessing. As the impure products of not-post-colonial 'North America' go crazy, 'Noone / bears witness for the / witness'; Noone drives the spewing car without licence. Yes and no ec-statically unsplit, singular-plural in the perverted body of the noem, there are appropriations and re-appropriations and other improper ways of making Noone('s) own (up); a poesis of acknowledgement and response-ability and honouring treaty.

The Red River Twang (also known as Bungee) was the dialect (now 'dead') used primarily by English speakers in the Red River Colony. Red River was the first European settlement sanctioned by the Hudson's Bay Company in the area then known as Rupert's Land. The Colony was paid for by Thomas Douglas, 5th Earl of Selkirk, and established in 1812 near the forks of the Red and Assiniboine rivers, where Winnipeg, Manitoba, now sits. The Red River Twang was a 'polyglot jabber' of Scots English and Cree, with vestiges of Gaelic and French. French was also spoken in the Colony, and some Métis people still speak Michif, a French-Cree creole using French nouns, Cree verbs and vocabulary from other local Indigenous languages. According to the Native Languages of the Americas website (www.native-languages.org), 'It's likely that Michif originated, not as a pidgin between Crees and Frenchmen trying to communicate with each other, but as a badge of identity and occasionally necessary secret code among Métis raised in both languages (similar to Yiddish in Europe).' Due to the intermixing of languages and cultures in the area, Cree became a *lingua franca* at the Red River Colony. As Red River settler J. J. Hargrove wrote in 1871, 'A man whose language is English, and one who speaks French alone, are enabled to render themselves mutually intelligible by means of Cree, their Indian mother tongue, though each is totally ignorant of the ... language ordinarily used by the other.'

Rev. John West was the first Protestant missionary in the 'Canadian North-West,' stationed at the Red River Settlement in 1820. West was also the first Protestant missionary to take Indigenous children away from their families, to be housed and schooled at the Red River Colony, as part of a 'policy of concentration' and cultural genocide. West wrote his own memoirs, and Rev. Bertal Heeney also wrote a fawning book on West's call to this Anglican 'civilizing' mission.

Rev. James Evans has been credited as the inventor of the Cree syllabics system, although this fact is contested. Some argue that the Creator gave the syllabics to the Cree people, and others argue that they were developed by the Cree people themselves – long before colonization. Some say there are rock rubbings in England that are evidence of the presence of syllabics long before white folks were about. The first book that Evans, 'the man who made birchbark talk,' translated into Cree syllabics was the Bible. Evans was also the first missionary in the 'Canadian North-West' to be tried (in a toothless church court) for sexual abuse of Indigenous children in his care – in 1846 at the Rossville Settlement in the territory now called Manitoba. A few words of testimony remain from the trial. Rev. Egerton Ryerson Young wrote a biography of Evans as the Methodist 'apostle of the north,' as well as an allegorical tale, 'Who is this Jesus?', about Evans's interactions with one Indigenous girl.

Rev. J. S. Woodsworth, first leader of the Co-operative Commonwealth Foundation (CCF), precursor to the NDP party, operated the All People's Mission in North End Winnipeg in the early part of the twentieth century. North End Winnipeg at that time was a slum or 'ghetto' where predominantly Eastern European immigrants lived and worked at the vast rail yards in the 'Gateway City to the West.' My grandfather, Falk Zolf, arrived in North End Winnipeg in 1929 to teach Yiddish to neighbourhood schoolchildren. Woodsworth wrote two well-known, openly white-supremacist, books, *Strangers Within Our Gates: Or, Coming Canadians* (1909) and *My Neighbor* (1911). Woodsworth's Methodist 'social gospel' mission was not markedly different from the American evangelical Youth for Christ's mission in the North End today (which is partly funded by Canadian municipal and federal governments), though the populace has shifted from immigrant to predominantly Indigenous. Youth for Christ's website once openly stated that Winnipeg's 'aboriginal youth community is a prime area for development.' The North End is still deemed a ghetto, and crime columns still brand people 'known to frequent the North End.' Yet, it is also possible, perhaps, to think of North End Winnipeg today as an Indigenous land-reclamation project.

'Vocabulary To Come' can be found on pages 534–538 in *Neiv Light on the early history of the Greater NorthJVest the Manuscript Journals of Alexander Henry Fur Trader of the Northwest Compatiy and of David Thompson Official Geographer and Explorer of the same Company 1799-I8I4* NeV\^ York Francis P. Harper 1897.

A one-week span lies between the hanging of Métis revolutionary Louis Riel and the last spike of the Canadian Pacific Railway (CPR) in November 1885, inextricably linked events that wrenched open the 'Canadian North-West' to mass European immigration. 'What [White] Women Say of the Canadian North-West' is a CPR immigration-recruitment pamphlet from 1886, a sequel to 'What Settlers [i.e., the white men] Say.' Both documents can be found in the Internet Archive (archive.org), along with most of the other texts exploited here.

Police documents now verify that close to 1,200 Indigenous women have been murdered or gone missing in the part of Turtle Island known as Canada in the last thirty years. Many of these women have roots in the territory now called Manitoba. Before its funding was cut by the federal government, the Native Women's Association of Canada gathered names of missing and murdered Indigenous mothers, daughters, aunties, granddaughters, lovers, sisters, cousins, grandmothers and friends. Amnesty International wrote a report; the RCMP wrote a report; and a PhD student, Maryanne Pearce, released a list of names bearing some of the misappellations and misappropriations that lists tend to produce. Yet, to date in 2014, no national public inquiry has been established to examine this systemic colonial violence against Indigenous women and children. And no national police task force has been launched to find the missing and bring some justice to the murdered. Genocidal colonial practices continue to place the lives of Indigenous women under erasure.

WHAT ELSE SAID AUTHOR ACKNOWLEDGES

I would like to acknowledge that I wrote this book while living on the traditional territories of the Niitsitapi, Nakoda and Tsuu t'ina peoples.

The concept of an Indigenous 'going on of life' that precedes and exceeds colonization comes from Daniel Heath Justice. Glen Coulthard's critique of the politics of recognition also resonates here.

Earlier versions of some poems appeared in the following publications: *Blackbox Manifold* (U.K.), *Lit* (U.S.), *Valve* (U.K.), *Dreamboat* (U.S.), *Capitalism Nature Socialism* (U.K.), *Arc/Cordite* (Canada/Australia), *Line, Capilano Review, Oscar's Salon* and as a chapbook by No Press. Thank you to the editors. The Canada Council for the Arts and the Social Sciences and Humanities Research Council (SSHRC) provided research funding. Many thanks to Alana Wilcox, Jeramy Dodds and the Coach House staff and printers.

I would like to acknowledge the invaluable assistance I received from the following people in the course of writing this book: Audrey Gardner, Victoria Freeman, Margaret Christakos, Robert Majzels, Sarah Dowling, Heather Milne, Fenn Stewart, Melissa Buzzeo, Peter Kulchyski, Christine Stewart, Carmen Derkson, Danielle LaFrance, Erika MacPherson, Roewan Crowe, Emily Beall, Diana Sherlock, Joan Retallack, Paul Seesequasis, Juliana Spahr, Jordan Scott, Shannon Maguire, Reena Katz, Gail Singer, Cheryl Sourkes, Divya Victor, Jeff T. Johnson, Moyra Davey, Kevin Killian, CAConrad, Aruna Srivastava, Laura Elrick, M. NourbeSe Philip, Amy De'Ath, Rita McKeough, Am Johal, Kate Eichhorn, Gregory Betts, Elena Basile, Gail Scott, Jeff Derksen, Colin Smith and Natalie Knight.

For their bodied inscriptions of grievable names and lives, special thanks to the scribes: Katherena Vermette, Rowan Furst, Ela Furst, Rosanna Deerchild, Kaydance, Raven, Bernadette Smith, Monique Woroniak, Nancy Tovell, Colleen Cawood, Ashlyn Haglund, Chandra Mayor, Anna Lundberg, Reuben Boulette, Cynthia Menzies, Lisa Gower and Leah Decter.

Christina Littlejohn

Sandi Lynn Malcolm

Tania Marsden

theresa Marsland

Dorothy Martin

Belinda McCay

Colleen McDonald

Jocelyn Chippy McDonald

Jamie McGuire

Roberta McIvor

Chloey McKay

Honey Joy McKay

Corrine McKeown

Leanne McLean

Paige Lektra Merrick-Klyne

Maggie Mink

Victoria Mink

Elaine Moar

Hailey Moar

Jean Mocharski

Glenda Morrisead

Marilyn Munroe

Irma Lynn Murdock

Tanya Nepinak

Breanne Oberman

Charlene Orshalak

Claudette Osborne-Tyo

Helen Betty Osborne

Betsy Owens

Precious Pascal

Sherry Paul

Valerie Ann Paypompee

Denise Pompana

Jaykene Redhead

Lorna Redhead

Simone Sanderson

Crystal Saunders

Sophia Schmidt

Geraldine Settee

Beatrice Sinclair

Caroline Sinclair

Lorraine Sinclair

Phoenix Sinclair

Tiffany Skye

Mary Smith.

Velicia Solomon-Osborne

Jacqueline Stanicia

Cindy Stevenson

EVELYN STEWART

Noreen Taylor

Cassandra Thomas

Heaven Traverse

Tatia Ulm

Jennifer Ward

Wilma Wasicuna

Gail Watt

Glenda Wesley

Hilary Angel Wilson

Marie Wood

Sunshine Wood

Annie Yassie

JUDY YOUNG

Typeset in Huronia.

Huronia, designed by Ross Mills between 2005 and 2011, is a massive type family that pushes the extents of the OpenType format by offering all Latin-based character sets, Greek, Cyrillic, Cree Syllabics, Cherokee and the International Phonetic Alphabet. These features make Huronia one of the largest and most versitle fonts available to designers around the world.

Printed at the Coach House on bpNichol Lane in Toronto, Ontario, on Zephyr Antique Laid paper, which was manufactured, acid-free, in Saint-Jérôme, Quebec, from second-growth forests. This book was printed with vegetable-based ink on a 1965 Heidelberg KORD offset litho press. Its pages were folded on a Baumfolder, gathered by hand, bound on a Sulby Auto-Minabinda and trimmed on a Polar single-knife cutter.

Edited by Jeramy Dodds
Designed by Alana Wilcox
Author photo by M. N. Hutchinson
Cover image from *Canada West – The New Homeland*, an immigration brochure distributed in Europe by the federal Department of Immigration and Colonization, Ottawa, 1930. Courtesy CP Archives.

Coach House Books
80 bpNichol Lane
Toronto ON M5S 3J4
Canada

416 979 2217
800 367 6360

mail@chbooks.com
www.chbooks.com